Cheer Up!

Dedicated to all wives and mothers who need strengthening and cheering in their powerful and influential calling to determine the destiny of nations.

More Titles from Prescott Publishing:

How to Encourage Your Children:
Tools to Help You Raise Mighty Warriors for God
By Nancy Campbell

How to Encourage Your Husband:
Ideas to Revitalize Your Marriage
by Nancy Campbell

Love Your Husband/Love Yourself:
Embracing God's Purpose for Passion in Marriage
by Jennifer Flanders

Cheer Up!

Motivating Messages
for Each Day of the Year

Nancy Campbell & Michelle Kauenhofen

Prescott Publishing

Cheer up!
by Nancy Campbell (Editress of *Above Rubies*) and
Michelle Kauenhoffen (Canadian Director of *Above Rubies*)
Copyright © January 2012, *Above Rubies*

Published in cooperation with Prescott Publishing in Tyler, TX
http://prescottpublishing.org

Cover design by Rachel Ramm
Dublin, Ohio, USA
rachel@rammnation.com

All Scriptures, unless otherwise stated, are taken from the King James
Version of the Bible. Abbreviated translations used are as follows:

ESV	English Standard Version
GNB	Good News Bible
MLB	Modern Language Bible
NASB	New American Standard Bible
NIV	New International Version
NKJB	New King James Version
NLT	New Living Translation

Above Rubies is a magazine devoted to strengthening and encouraging marriage,
motherhood, and family life. Nancy Campbell has been publishing *Above Rubies* for
over 34 years, and it currently goes to over 100 countries worldwide. To receive this
life-changing magazine, which is available by donation, go to www.aboverubies.org
or email your address to nancy@aboverubies.org.

To view resources of books, manuals, DVDs, CDs and music recordings to
encourage you in your high calling, go to the *Book & Music Store* at
http://bit.ly/AboveRubiesBookStore

To read hundreds of articles on subjects relating to marriage, motherhood and family
life go to www.aboverubies.org and click on *Articles and Stories*.

To receive an encouraging *Weekly Email* for wives and mothers, send a blank email
to subscribers-on@aboverubies.org

To join the *Above Rubies Facebook*, type in "Above Rubies."
Come in each morning to receive a positive and encouraging word to help you
through your day of mothering and training the next generation. Or go to:
http://bit.ly/aboverubiesblog

Men who want an uncompromising Facebook for men, type in "Meat for Men."
Or go to: http://bit.ly/MeatforMenBlog

ISBN: 9780982626993

- Introduction -

The following inspirational writings are Facebook posts which Michelle Kauenhoffen and I post each day on the Above Rubies Facebook. These posts are forgotten as they disappear with new posts appearing each day. Plus, there are many women who are not yet on Facebook. Therefore, we are making them available for you as a Daily Devotional.

One Facebook reader states, "After my Bible reading each day, yours and Michelle's Facebook posts are what I most look forward to reading."

You will read one from Michelle and one from me for each day of the year. Each morning you can open this book and be refueled for the day as you prepare to accomplish your divine task of being a loving wife and mother in your home. These short inspirations won't take long to read but they will be enough to give you a shot in the arm to start the day.

I trust that "God, who cheers the depressed" will comfort and inspire you. I pray that as you face another year, maybe with unknown challenges ahead, that God will cheer your heart in the midst of whatever you face.

I admit that some messages may challenge you more than cheer you, but as you open your heart to new understanding that God speaks to you, I know you will be lifted up to a higher plane and ultimately cheered up! We will never live in a state of cheerfulness while we stay in a rut, and yet, without constant challenge in our lives, that's often where we stay.

Cheerful reading!

Nancy Campbell
www.aboverubies.org

- January 1 -

I Belong to the Lord

Isaiah 44:5 NASB says, *"This one will say, 'I am the Lord's'; and that one will call on the name of Jacob; and another will write on his hand, 'Belonging to the Lord,'"*

What a wonderful way to start the year with the affirmation, *"I belong to the Lord."* My every thought should be overshadowed with the words, *"I belong to the Lord."* Every decision I make should be influenced by the fact that I am owned by the Lord. Everything I say should be inspired by the fact that I no longer live for myself, but unto God.

I wrote the words, *"I belong to the Lord"* on my hand this morning. Then, I wrote it on the hands of my grandchildren. They loved it. *Nancy*

New Habits

The New Year is a great time to reflect on our own growth. It dawned on me today that if I established one new habit each month, I could have 12 new habits by the year's end! I need to be intentional and I know where I need to start. We are quite diligent with Family Devotions at our supper table, but not so great at breakfast time. We need to re-establish this in our home as it seems to have slipped away over the last couple of years. New habits are easy to form with some intention and effort! I am excited to develop new habits and new purposes. Will you join me? *Michelle*

- January 2 -

God First

Psalm 124:8 says, *"Our help is in the name of the Lord, who made heaven and earth."*

Where do you go to get help? Do you run to man's wisdom, or to God? When something is broken or goes wrong, isn't it best to go the original maker? That's the one who really has the answer.

How wonderful that we can cry out to God who made heaven and earth and who made every intricate part of our body. Let's get into the habit of coming to God FIRST! He will give us the right help. *Nancy*

New Every Morning

It's a New Year! The beginning of a new month! A new day! I like the word "new!" We don't have to live our old life; we can be new! We are not the same; we are changed (II Corinthians 5:17)!

We are not stuck in our same sinful patterns, for *"His compassions fail not. They are new every morning: great is Thy faithfulness"* (Lamentations 3:22-23).

We can start afresh this New Year and see great new things! *Michelle*

- January 3 -

To the Guttermost!

A mother shared, "I can't do another year like this last one. It will kill me."

If you feel like this as you face another year, may I encourage you that no matter how far into the depths you may go, God will go further? He saves *"to the uttermost"* (Hebrews 7:25). One preacher said, *"to the guttermost!"* His everlasting arms are underneath you, no matter how far you sink (Deuteronomy 33:27).

Thank Him and rest in His unfailing love. Be encouraged too, that this life is only a vapor. Every hard and difficult trial you are going through is working for you a *"far more exceeding and eternal weight of glory"* (II Corinthians 4:17-18). *Nancy*

Touch of Sweetness

A touch of honey sweetens so many things and makes them taste delightful. I love a tad of raw honey in my tea! It is also true with our words. A touch of sweetness can change the whole direction of a conversation, the whole ambiance of a room, the whole attitude of a family, the whole thought process of a person, and the whole direction of a relationship. It even brings health!

Proverbs 16:24 reads, *"Pleasant words are as an honeycomb, sweet to the soul, and health to the bones."* Be sweet today. Sweetness equals multiple blessings. *Michelle*

- January 4 -

The Path of Blessing

Do you want the blessing of God upon your life throughout this year? Do you want your children to be blessed? God does not keep us in the dark about how to go about it. He informs us that families will be blessed who do not *"walk in the counsel of the ungodly, nor stand in the way of sinners, nor sit in the seat of the scornful"* (Psalm 1:1).

This means we will do everything in our power to make sure our children do not receive ungodly teaching. We certainly would not want them to sit for many hours a day and be educated by those who may scorn God's Word and His ways. Likewise, we wouldn't think of allowing our young *"olive plants"* to hang out every day with those who will influence them toward evil rather than righteousness.

Instead, let's seek the path of God's blessing for this coming year. *Nancy*

I'm Free

Nancy writes in her book, *100 Days of Blessing*, that if you only do what is required of you, you are a slave; yet if you do more than is required, you are FREE.

Isn't that so true? We are completely free to do more than is required of us! In fact, it is not only freeing, but gratifying to do more than is required! Enjoy your day of freedom. *Michelle*

My Mission

You might like to type out this *Mission Statement for Mothers* and pin it up in your kitchen to remind yourself. I am...

M Mothering with passion!
I Inviting God into every situation I face today!
S Serving with joy, even in the routine and mundane!
S Saturating my husband & children with love & encouragement!
I Intercepting the devil's attacks with prayer and praise!
O Overflowing with joy and thankfulness!
N Nurturing my children with God's anointing!

"Thank you, Lord, for the privilege of being part of the greatest mission on earth. Amen." *Nancy*

A Child's Reminder

My six-year-old asked me how cold it was going to be outside. I went to the computer and said, "Let's see what the weather says."

"You mean what God says!" she corrected.

Yes, that is what I meant. She understands that God controls all things, even the weather. The computer would only tell me what God was doing with the weather.

Don't you love it when your children teach you or remind you of the truth? *Michelle*

- January 6 -

Be of Good Cheer

God will not forsake you in the storms of life. This is when He delights to come to your aid. When the disciples were in the midst of the storm and battered by the waves, Jesus came. What were His words? *"Be of good cheer; it is I; be not afraid"* (Matthew 14:27). The true meaning of the word "cheer" is to "take courage."

If someone tells you to "take courage" in the storm, you may think, "What do you know about what I am going through?" But when Jesus says, *"Be of good cheer,"* you can take courage because He, the Creator of the universe, is backing His words.

No matter how fierce the storm in your life, God is bigger. You may drown on your own, but when God comes and brings His cheer and courage, you'll weather the storm! You no longer have to fear because He is with you. *Nancy*

Training Tips

Teaching biblical concepts in daily life to children at all age levels is challenging. Here are two of my favorite family exhortations when training children.

1) "If it's not fun for all, it's not fun at all." I say this when someone is being left out or mistreated.

2) "If you show it, you share it." This helps them to consider others when they have a treat or want a treat. *Michelle*

- January 7 -

No Longer Groveling

Are you groveling or girding? Colossians 3:2-3 Way's translation says, *"Let your thoughts dwell on things above, not grovel on the earth."* God does not want us to grovel in self-pity and depression. He wants us to gird up the loins of our minds (I Peter 1:13).

In Bible days, to keep from being hindered, people lifted up their long robes and tucked them into their belt if they were planning to do something really active. In the same way, we have to gird up our minds and get rid of all negative thoughts that hinder us from walking in victory.

Negative, self-pitying, unbelieving thoughts may constantly come to your mind, but YOU DON'T HAVE TO ENTERTAIN THEM! YOU DON'T HAVE TO GROVEL IN THEM! Rebuke them in the name of Jesus and begin praising the Lord and quoting Scripture. *Nancy*

Happy Chores

The other day I told my husband I needed some inspiration about what to write to the mothers. He replied, "I should be your inspiration!"

Today he really is the inspiration. I just heard him tell our nine-year-old son to do a particular chore. Then I heard him sing a little tune he made up, *"Be happy, be happy, it helps you do your chore. Be happy, be happy, and don't complain no mooore!"* I think we shall all start singing that around here a lot more often. It is the new Kauenhofen family favorite! I wish all of you could have heard it! *Michelle*

- January 8 -

What Will You Wear Today?

What are you wearing today? Your "down in the dumps" dress, your "grumble groaning" dress, or, maybe your "self-pity" outfit? Pretty ugly, aren't they?

Did you know that God gave you a new wardrobe when He came to live in you? He wants you to cast off the old clothes of the flesh and put on the new clothes He has given you—kindness, joy, mercy, humility, longsuffering, love, and forgiveness. These clothes make you look very beautiful, especially to your husband and children. You can choose to wear the drab "fleshly" clothes of your old life or the new clothes of the Spirit, which God has given to you at the great cost of His life.

Ephesians 4: 24 says, *"**Put on** the new man, which after God is created in righteousness and true holiness."* Do you need to change your clothes? Won't you look lovely in your "pretty patience outfit" or perhaps your new "joyful dress"? It will change the whole vibe of your home. *Nancy*

The Best Book

I was sitting in my dimly lit room pondering the depths of Psalm 107:33-43, when my 11-year-old son walked in and saw me with the Bible in my lap. As he passed my doorway, he lifted up his right hand as though to add impact to his statement and said with vigor, "The best book in the world!"

That's right, my son, that's right! *Michelle*

- January 9 -

From Misery to Joy

What brings gladness to your home? The psalmist tells us his secret. *"There is a river, the streams whereof shall make glad the city of God, the holy place of the tabernacles of the most High"* (Psalm 46:4).

In the Bible the river speaks of the Holy Spirit (John 7:37-38). When you allow the Holy Spirit to fill your heart and your home, He brings joy and gladness.

Turn aside from the flesh and let the Holy Spirit have control. You'll be amazed how the atmosphere in your home will change from misery to joy. *Nancy*

Let Them See

I think it is good for children to see that their parents are truly in love and desiring each other's company. One of my daughters saw this when my husband inadvertently sent a text message to her phone that was meant for me! Oops! On the bright side, she clearly knows there are still flames in her parent's marriage!

Although this type of incident is not recommended, do make sure your children know that you are "still in love" by your words and deeds. Let them see you kiss and embrace, but try not to let them see your texts! *Michelle*

Prayer on Prayer

How do you stand strong without going under? How do you stand strong in the Lord when you feel weak? How do you stand strong when people oppose what you are doing?

Way's translation of Ephesians 6:18, which summarizes verses 10-17, reads, *"So stand, praying the while with prayer on prayer, with petition on petition, at every season, stirred by the Spirit."* Prayer is the answer.

Philippians 4:6 says, *"In every thing by prayer and supplication with thanksgiving let your requests be made known unto God."* Did you notice that it is not some things, but everything?

Bring EVERY need to God in prayer. Instead of sighing, PRAY! When overwhelmed, PRAY! When you don't know what to do, PRAY! It's not one prayer, but *"prayer on prayer."* Become a "walking prayer meeting," as my husband encourages us all. *Nancy*

Follow Christ's Example

Isn't it strange how opposite our culture is to the example Jesus set? He said, *"Let the children come to Me. Don't stop them! For the Kingdom of Heaven belongs to such as these"* (Matthew 19:14 NLT). Yet, our society continually looks for ways to get the children out of our way. Enjoy every child that crosses your path today, and in this way you will follow Christ's example. *Michelle*

Our Crowning Moment

What is the crowning moment of your day? For me, it is sitting down to the evening meal, enjoying rich fellowship, and then the culminating moment—Family Devotions when we read God's Word and pray together.

It makes the meal preparation all worthwhile. It crowns the day with God's blessing. I am always aware of the power and impact it has, not only on our lives, but on the people and nations for whom we pray!

Try not to let the interruptions of this day keep you from this crowning moment. *Nancy*

A Little Sunshine

I was trying in vain to thread a very tiny needle to do a mending job, which is one of my least favorite chores. I thought of asking one of the children to do it for me, but realized I should not be such a quitter. I moved to a sunny spot, and just as smooth as silk, that thread went right through on the first try.

I told the children that all I needed was a little sunshine! It is so true— a touch of sunshine, a brighter perspective, and a more joyful attitude can make things that seem as rough as sandpaper turn out as smooth as silk! *Michelle*

Reign in Life

Romans 4:17 talks about *"reigning in life."* Where do you reign? In the domain where you live which is your home. Are you reigning over the frustrations of this day? Anger? Unforgiveness? Confusion? You don't have to give into these emotions. You were saved to reign!

You ask how? Only one way. Through Christ Jesus! Instead of giving in to your feelings, thank the Lord Jesus Christ that He lives in you; and therefore, all the good things that are in Christ are in you! That's a fact! Acknowledge it.

Instead of reacting in anger, confess aloud, "Thank you, Jesus, for your patience which dwells in me. I am reigning in patience." Allow Him to live His life through you and REIGN! Will your husband come home tonight to a reigning wife? I'm sure he will! *Nancy*

A Heart on Fire

Does your heart burn within you? I hope so! I hope it burns with excitement when the Lord opens up a Scripture to you. The disciples on the way to Emmaus exclaimed, *"Did not our heart burn within us, while He talked with us by the way, and while He opened to us the Scriptures?"* (Luke 24:32).

I also hope your heart burns with passion for your spouse (if you're married)! A heart on fire will guard our lives from becoming complacent—both spiritually and relationally. Love God and love your husband passionately. This is an exciting life. No longer boring! *Michelle*

- January 13 -

Life is a Boomerang

Life is a like a boomerang. Everything we do comes back to us. The more love, forgiveness, kindness, smiles, and blessings we pour out on others, the more those things come back to us. Have you lost a loved one and experienced God's comfort? Have you gone through a trial and experienced God's faithfulness and comfort? Pour out the comfort you have experienced on others (II Corinthians 1:3-4).

Everything God gives to us should be given to others. We are not an island unto ourselves. Everything we say and do will affect our husband, children, and others either negatively or positively. Correspondingly, we will reap either negatively or positively. Pour out on your husband, children, and others all the good things God gives you. *Nancy*

Give Others Hope

I love II Corinthians 1:3-4 about comforting others with the comfort we have been given. When we go through a trial and come out the other side, we are able to comfort others going through a similar hardship because of our experience.

We can give others hope because we have seen first-hand how the Lord carried us through. When we face trials, we are being equipped to comfort others. Not only we, but others, see how the Lord takes care of us through hard times! *Michelle*

In the Morning

Talking about Jerusalem, Psalm 46:5 says, *"God shall help her, and that right early."* The New English Bible says *"at the break of day"* and another translation says, *"when morning dawns."* When you are going through trouble and everything seems impossibly dark, bleak and drear, remember that God brings His deliverance in the morning!

Don't take your worries to bed with you. Give them to the Lord. While you sleep, God will work on your behalf. He will give you His help in the morning. Do you need to overcome? Psalm 49:14 says, *"The upright shall have dominion over them **in the morning**."* Do you need comfort? Lamentations 3:22-23 tells us that God's mercies and compassion are *"new **every morning**."* *Nancy*

In Spite of Circumstances

In Hebrews 13:15-16 ESV we see that God is still pleased with sacrifice! *"Through Him then let us continually offer up a sacrifice of praise to God, that is, the fruit of lips that acknowledge His name. Do not neglect to do good and to share what you have, for such sacrifices are pleasing to God."*

It's easy to praise God when things are going well. It's also easy to do good and share when there is an abundance. This involves no real sacrifice! It is a sacrifice to praise God, to do good, and to share when things are not going well and when there is no abundance. Let's please God today with our praise and sharing, no matter what our circumstances! *Michelle*

- January 15 -

Strengthened in the Fight

Do you feel weak in the battle? You wonder if you'll ever make it through? Don't despair. The great heroes of the faith felt weak too.

But, Hebrews 11:34 tells us that from their weakness they became strong in the battle and mighty in war! The KJV says that they "*waxed valiant in fight.*" They didn't start off strong, but as they fought their battles, they gradually became stronger.

You don't become strong sitting on the sidelines. You become stronger with each battle you fight. *Nancy*

See the Unity

"Master, we saw one casting out devils in Thy name; and we forbade him, because he followeth not with us. And Jesus said unto him, Forbid him not: for he that is not against us is for us" (Luke 9:49-50).

I love this Scripture! Sometimes we are prone to look at all the places we are different from each other instead of looking at what we have in common! The disciples saw the differences, but Jesus saw the similarities!

We are all different members but the same body. *Michelle*

Multiplied Strength

II Chronicles 20:13 says, *"And all Judah stood before the Lord, with their little ones, their wives, and their children."* Include your children in your walk with God. Don't send them off to be influenced by the peers of their age group. Grow in God together as a family.

Proverbs 22:15 says, *"Foolishness is bound in the heart of a child."* When you put a lot of children of the same age together, you have multiplied foolishness!

God intends us to follow after Him as "families," not in separated age groups. This makes strong families for God; and when we have multiplied strong families, the nation will be strong. *Nancy*

Bright Spots on Hard Days

My daughter requested that I buy baguettes for her. However, I decided we should make our own with spelt and eat healthier. We found a recipe, got adventurous, and made the baguettes, but as they were baking, I added water to the pan at the bottom of the stove and cracked the glass on the inside of my oven door because it was so hot! Suddenly, 99-cent-store-bought baguettes looked like a better option! Within the hour, my husband walked in with flowers for me—"just because" flowers! He had no idea what I had done and how crummy I was feeling. The Lord is so gracious to give us bright spots on hard days. Some are not as obvious, but when we look they are always there—a smile, a touch, a kind word or deed, and sometimes—even flowers! *Michelle*

- January 17 -

Right Thinking

What are you teaching your children? It's easy to get into the mode of packing information into your children's brains—the more the better! But "information" is not education. "Right thinking" is education. Unless your children know how to think correctly, information won't do them a lot of good.

Right thinking comes from God's Word—even though it is often contrary to how society thinks and what is taught in the public education system.

Isaiah 55:8-9 says, *"For My thoughts are not your thoughts, neither are your ways My ways, saith the Lord. For as the heavens are higher than the earth, so are My ways higher than your ways, and My thoughts than your thoughts."*

To truly educate your children, you must give them the right foundation, which is GOD-THINKING, not humanistic thinking! *Nancy*

Try Again!

I haven't failed! I have just given myself an opportunity to get up and have a new start. How exciting is that? With all this practice, it's bound to get perfect. *Michelle*

- January 18 -

A Day of Good Things

What are the older women to teach the younger women? GOOD THINGS. Titus 2:3-5 tells us that to love your husband, love your children, and to be a keeper at home, etc., are "good" things. As you seek to manage your home efficiently, and to nurture and train your children today, you are doing a GOOD THING! It's not a boring thing. It's not an insignificant thing. It's a GOOD THING!

Ephesians 6:8 says, *"Whatsoever good thing any man doeth, the same shall he receive of the Lord."* What a beautiful promise. We don't look for rewards, but God's law says that we reap what we sow. As you joyfully carry out these "good" works in your home, they will boomerang back on you. You will reap God's blessings (I Corinthians 15:58). You will not lose. You will win! *Nancy*

Family Play Dough

It is so wonderful to watch children having a good time! The other day, our 11-year-old made two colors of homemade play dough for a mere few cents!

What an economical way to keep all of the children happy! Seven children played for the entire evening, wowing Mom and Dad with their magnificent creations! Everyone went to bed in great spirits and with their love tanks full!

Need a lovely family night? Whip up some play dough! *Michelle*

Diligently!

Not only does God call mothering and homemaking a *"good"* thing (Titus 2:3-5 and I Timothy 5:10), but there's something else! He also tells us *how* to do these good things!

How do you think we should do them? Grudgingly? Reluctantly? Complainingly? No, the word is *"diligently"*! Do you want to know the real meaning of the word? The Greek is *akribo*s, and it literally means "perfectly, exactly, and circumspectly." No room for slovenliness! No room for half-heartedness! No room for sloppiness!

Don't forget who you are working for today—the King of kings and Lord of lords! That sets the tone, doesn't it? *Nancy*

Spread the Joy

"Neither be ye sorry; for the joy of the Lord is your strength" (Nehemiah 8:10). It takes no strength to complain or be grumpy. It takes no strength to sit in self-pity. It takes great strength to stand in joy, regardless of the circumstances. It takes amazing strength to rejoice rather than grumble.

God is pleased to offer this strength to us at every moment. We can consciously walk in His joy. We mustn't wait for our feelings or circumstances to line up in order for us to walk in joy. It is a powerful testimony to be joyful, and it is magnetic. Everyone wants it. It doesn't matter what is going on, we can still have the joy of the Lord! Spread the joy! *Michelle*

- January 20 -

An Amazing Life

"I wish I had a life!" I often hear mothers making this statement. Dear mother, you HAVE A LIFE! An amazing life! The most important career in the nation! You are training godly children to impact this nation for God. You couldn't spend your life in a more important vocation! Deuteronomy 32:46-47 says, *"Command your children to observe to do, all the words of this law. For it is not a vain thing for you; because IT IS YOUR LIFE."*

Your greatest vocation in life is to diligently mother and teach your children in the ways and commandments of the Lord. It's a full time career! Not one minute with your children will be wasted. It is not a vain thing. It has eternal value. Every day you are not only preparing children to impact this world, but you are molding them for eternity. *Nancy*

The Power of the Apron

I was inspired by the picture of a 1950's housewife all dolled up and donning a cute apron to take on her domestic duties. It prompted me to purchase several aprons of various sizes and colors from our local secondhand shop. You wouldn't believe the motivation these little aprons brought! Within moments of coming in the door, three daughters had donned aprons. One hour later, they were still joyfully cleaning, brooms in hand!

I am wearing one, too, and my living room is completely tidied and reconfigured. On to the next room! The power of the apron! Highly recommended for making a house a lovely home! *Michelle*

- January 21 -

Lay a Foundation

Because I have memorized Deuteronomy 32:46-47, I am still meditating on this Scripture. It's easy to meditate on a Scripture when you have memorized it, isn't it? The first words say, *"Set your hearts..."* The Hebrew word, *sum,* means "to establish, to plant, to put down, to lay in." To set our hearts to God's Words means that we will make sure they are planted in our hearts and our minds are fixed toward them.

Because this is our attitude, it will be *"our life"* to diligently implant God's Word into our children's hearts. If we have a set course, we will not be double minded. We will not send them to Sunday school on Sunday, and then into state education for the next five days of the week where they will be taught beliefs that contradict what we teach them at home. How can we be DOUBLE MINDED in setting our hearts to command our children in the ways of God? *Nancy*

Liberated!

I feel liberated! I awoke to the sound of my children, not an alarm. I dressed according to my plans for the day, not someone else's. I donned my apron, cleaned my home, made nutritious meals in between teaching my children what I wanted them to learn. I was free to exercise, chat, laugh, train, teach, and enjoy my children, my home and God's provisions. Some think I need liberation from my home and children to feel free. Where did they get that idea? I am completely free and liberated (and even a tad spoiled) to be home! *Michelle*

- January 22 -

Not a Suggestion

I notice in Deuteronomy 32:46-47 that it is not optional to teach our children God's Word. We are admonished to *"COMMAND your children to observe to do, all the words of this law."* We must diligently penetrate God's Word into their hearts. This is our LIFE, remember?

I am reminded of God's blessing on Abraham. God said, *"I know him, that he will COMMAND HIS CHILDREN and his household after him, and they shall keep the way of the Lord, to do justice and judgment"* (Genesis 18:18-19). I personally know a mother who has her own personal relationship with God. However, she has never commanded her children to follow the Lord. She never took them to church. Now they are grown and some are not walking in God's kingdom; one particularly walks in the depths of sin. Your children won't automatically walk in God's ways. It has to be your LIFE to command them. *Nancy*

Living the Dream

If you are like me, you grew up playing with baby dolls and playing house. The best fun was to play with dolls and pretend we were a mother with our own home and children to care for. Now, we have real live babies and a real home to care for! What a delight! How many people get to do in their adult lives what they always loved to do for entertainment?

If you care for children and the home, not only do you "have a life," but you are "living the dream!" *Michelle*

Most Loved Word

"Mom," "Mamma," or whatever name signifies "Mother" to you is the word we must hear more than any other word in our lives as mothers. I love to hear it, don't you? When I am somewhere in public and hear someone calling "Mom," I still automatically go to respond. It is instinctive!

I was with some of the grandchildren this morning. "Nana!" "Nana, look!" "Nana, watch me!" comes from eight different directions at once. I am not sure where to look first as each child wants to show me what they can do or how they can climb the highest tree or swing from a branch from one tree to another like a monkey! I've even had to precariously climb a high tree where they are building a fort! What fun! *Nancy*

Let Me Hear It All My Life

I love being called upon, paged, needed, longed for, and hugged all day long by various-aged children! I love having them with me at every meal and every morning, afternoon, and evening!

Why do so many people think this is crazy? By my "crazy" standards, this is the best way to live life.

Let me hear "Mummy, Mom, Mum, Mummeee!" for all of my days! The fertile years pass way too fast for my liking. Do you love motherhood like crazy? *Michelle*

- January 24 -

Send It Kicking

When we eradicate evil in our home, we mustn't only sweep it outside the door. We must make sure we send it FAR FROM OUR HOME! Job 22:23-25 NASB says, *"If you return to the Almighty, you will be restored; if you remove unrighteousness **far from your tent** (your home)... then the Almighty will be your gold and choice silver to you."*

When Moses told Pharaoh that he was taking the children of Israel from Egypt to offer sacrifices to the Lord, he stated emphatically that they would not just go over the border, but they would go a THREE DAY JOURNEY out of Egypt (Exodus 3:18; 5:3; 8:27-28)!

Don't compromise with evil and the worldly spirit. Don't let it hang around the door of your home! Kick it FAR AWAY. *Nancy*

Keep Refilling!

I wondered to myself why it is that my children always empty things but never throw out the packaging. I then thought that it is a mother's privilege to keep filling what gets emptied, especially the children's love tanks and their fragile self-esteem.

I threw out the empty packaging with a smile and looked around for more hearts to refill. There is always a smile, a hug, a loving touch, an encouraging word, a word of praise, and a word of gratitude to offer to help fill up our children as they empty out in daily life. *Michelle*

Decisions Affect Descendants

"Seek for all the commandments of the Lord your God: that ye may possess this good land, and leave it for an inheritance for your children after you forever" (I Chronicles 28:8). Every decision we make and everything we do will have implications on the generations to come. If we seek after the Lord and follow His commandments, we can claim the promise that God will bless our progeny.

"Father, help us to walk in the fear of the Lord in our daily life and in our marriage relationship. Help us to make every decision with the understanding that it will not only affect our children today, but our grandchildren and descendents for years to come. Amen." *Nancy*

Healthy and Normal

I was thinking about the word "confinement" in regards to pregnancy. It originates from the thought that women should be confined in bed during pregnancy.

At times, we still see pregnancy as part inconvenience or part health risk when there is no need to view it as such. This creates fear and apprehension when, most of the time, pregnancies and deliveries are beautifully healthy and normal. This is so true that even after a complicated pregnancy and birth, the same woman can go on to have a most amazingly healthy and uncomplicated birth!

I have experienced 16 pregnancies and 11 births—some easy, some difficult, some risky and some not; and I still say, "Lord, confine me, please!" I cannot think of a better way to be "confined!" *Michelle*

- January 26 -

Ready for Marriage

Don't you love weddings? Recently my husband and I attended the wedding of a very young couple—the bride only 18 years old and the bridegroom barely 20! Were they ready for marriage? Yes, perhaps more ready than many older couples. It's not the age, but the maturity that counts. Many brides fall in love but are not ready in their mind for marriage and motherhood. They have been trained for other careers. Everyone at this wedding felt the presence of God and the SMILE AND FAVOR OF GOD. We realized why when the bride gave a speech at the reception. I'll tell you about it tomorrow. *Nancy*

Grateful for Blessings

"Godliness with contentment is great gain" (1 Timothy 6:6). By contrast, godliness without contentment is a great drain! It can be so easy to be discontent with our circumstances, can't it?

I live in a hostile climate for a large chunk of each year, and tend to become very discontent. I have been asking the Lord to help me embrace winter and my location. He showed me how lovely it is that I can buy spelt, sea salt, and grain at wholesale prices just down the road. I can buy our meat directly from a trustworthy farmer. We also have raw honey, fresh cheese, and raw milk conveniently and reasonably priced nearby. Not to mention the wonderful people we have in our lives.

Are His provisions in this place not amazing? I may not have warmth year round, but I have much that makes up for it! Are you counting your blessings today? *Michelle*

- January 27 -

God's Favor

Why was God's favor on this young couple? The service was beautiful—they married outside in the late evening with the last rays of the sun shining upon them. But that wasn't the reason. At the reception, there were many speeches from family and friends to bless the young couple. But after the speech of the day from the bridegroom, the young bride also spoke.

She shared many things, but the line that touched everyone's heart was the following: "I want to be his wife... I want to bear his children." She entered marriage with the understanding of God's highest purpose for her to bring forth godly seed. She was surrendered to God's plan instead of resisting it. Everyone felt the favor of God.

The night of the wedding, seven beautiful young ladies stayed at our home. They talked into the hours of the morning discussing everything about the wedding, and yes, THAT LINE! That's what got to them! *Nancy*

You Are Mine

Remember that special moment when you first held your precious newborn and called him by name? The adoration and overflow of love you felt? The overwhelming sense of protection that overtook you? These emotions come from the heart of God. He says in Isaiah 43:1, *"I have called thee by thy name; thou art Mine."* Our Father named us. He loves us even more than we can comprehend! Isn't that unbelievably comforting and encouraging? *Michelle*

- January 28 -

Tell the World

Psalm 107:2 reads, *"Let the redeemed of the Lord say so, whom He hath redeemed from the hand of the enemy."* In other words, the Psalmist says, "Come on, stop being so reticent. Let's tell the world about God's goodness and His amazing redemption!" If we really are the redeemed, we'll talk of Christ and His truths wherever we go—in the home to our children and to people we meet in the supermarket.

We named our daughter Evangeline, which means "the bearer of the good tidings of the gospel." From the time she was little we told her the meaning of her name and she grew up knowing it was her destiny. If I happen to enter a shop and see her there, she will be doing more than shopping. I will hear her telling "God stories" to everyone she meets. It doesn't matter who they are, rich or poor, believers or unbelievers, she tells them about the miracles of God in her life and her children's lives.

Let's tell the world! *Nancy*

Enjoy the Moments

"Jesus answered and said unto her, 'Martha, Martha, thou art careful and troubled about many things: but one thing is needful: and Mary hath chosen that good part, which shall not be taken away from her'" (Luke 10:41-42).

Martha is caught up in things that aren't that big of a deal, while Mary enjoys the moment. Instead of fretting, let's enjoy the moments. Today. *Michelle*

Even When Difficult

The Roman believers *"obeyed from the heart"* the doctrine which was given to them (Romans 6:17). When we obey from the heart, we will be committed to the truth no matter what. We will continue to walk in truth even when the way is difficult. Even when it seems too hard.

When we obey from the head, it is easy to give up when trials come and change to a doctrine that is more suitable to our circumstances. We become victims to "situational ethics" rather than victors for the truth. May God save us from being believers who are *"tossed to and fro, and carried about with every wind of doctrine"* (Ephesians 4:14), but rather mold us into believers who passionately obey from the heart. *Nancy*

Not Feelings, but Obedience

"You shall not wrong one another, but you shall fear your God; for I am the Lord your God" (Leviticus 25:17 ESV).

Sometimes in marriage (or other relationships), doing what is right before God is very difficult. We may be unable to do it out of love for the person because there is too much hurt. The great news is that we CAN do it out of obedience to our God!

If we wait until we feel like it, or for the person to deserve it, it may never happen. We do it out of obedience, with His help, and we trust the Lord to bless it. *Michelle*

- January 30 -

Obedience First

"To obey is better than sacrifice, and to hearken than the fat of rams" (1 Samuel 15:22). Just as obedience is necessary for our lives, so it is necessary for our children. If we want them to be purified by the Holy Spirit and grow into the image of Christ, they must learn obedience. How will they learn? They learn from watching our obedient spirit.

They learn as we teach and expect obedience from them. It is the foundational principle of parenting. If we are not faithful to teach our children to obey, how can we expect them to obey God and to grow into His likeness? *Nancy*

Fruit of the Spirit

At our family meal table tonight, the topic of fruit of the Spirit came up. We would sure like to see more fruit in our home! We put up charts for each one—love, joy, peace, patience, faith, kindness, goodness, gentleness and self-control. Each chart has every family member's name on it with room for stickers. Perhaps we shall see more fruit with the charts lined up in our dining room, as we all watch for them! At the very least, all of the children will have them memorized! *Michelle*

Shut Your Mouth

Why can't we stop talking? "But, God, I can't see how we can manage financially!" "But, God, I can't cope with everything I have to do!" "But, God, why do we have to continue going through this trial? It's been too long." We keep on complaining and confessing our lack of trust in God.

When the children of Israel faced the impossible—the sea in front of them with the Egyptians galloping behind to wipe them out, God said, *"Fear ye not, stand still, and see the salvation of the Lord... The Lord shall fight for you, and ye shall **hold your peace"*** (Exodus 14:13-14). In other words, God told them to keep quiet and to stop griping and speaking fear. Instead, trust in Him.

When we can't see a way out, or we can't think of anything positive to say, the best thing is to say nothing! Your negative words will bind you to your situation. Shut your mouth and see what God will do. *Nancy*

Take a Check

I often ask myself, "Am I thankful today for all that I have, or am I bitter about all I don't have?" This question is a healthy attitude check. Where is your focus today? Do you have an attitude of gratitude, or a bad attitude? *Michelle*

- February 1 -

Fruit of Loving Jesus

What is the fruit of loving Jesus? After Jesus had risen from the dead, He went down to Lake Galilee to fellowship with His disciples. Do you remember how He personally asked Peter, *"Lovest thou Me?"* Then He said to him, *"Feed My sheep... Feed My lambs"* (John 21:15-17).

The first response of our loving Jesus is to feed His sheep and lambs. God has given you precious lambs to protect and feed. The food for the lambs is the same as the sheep. We must daily lead them to good pasture, feeding them with the unadulterated Word of God.

The fruit of your loving Jesus does not mean you have to leave your home and get involved in some ministry. It is feeding your little lambs, spiritually and physically, right in your home. Be a good shepherdess today. *Nancy*

Redeem the Moments

Today, I hung a plaque on my wall which says, "Make each day your Masterpiece. We don't remember days, we remember moments." I especially like the part about remembering moments. We can blow everything in one moment and, in another, everything can be restored! We can have a sour moment, and then the next moment make the sweetest memory! Days are never write-offs. They are made up of many redeemable moments. Seize every one of them and be blessed as you bless. *Michelle*

- February 2 -

Your Greatest Blessing

The greatest blessing you can have in your home is the presence of the Lord. When the ark of the Lord (which represents the presence and glory of God) was in the house of Obed-edom the Gittite for three months, the Bible says that *"the Lord blessed Obed-edom, and all his household"* (II Samuel 6:11).

More than material possessions, more than making sure every school subject is finished each day, more than keeping up with the Joneses, seek after the presence of God. This will impact the lives of your children more than anything else in this world.

Will the atmosphere of the presence of God that permeates your home be the greatest memory your children take with them into their future? *Nancy*

Baby Lover

As we drove home from grocery shopping, Havenne, my 10-year-old said randomly, "Even if I can have babies myself, I will still adopt some. I will adopt in between having my own so I won't have to wait so long to hold a baby." We have a baby lover on our hands. I think she might be getting impatient waiting for me to get pregnant. Hopefully soon! *Michelle*

- February 3 -

Tune Your Ears

What are you listening to? The spirit of this world? Your own feelings and fleshly thoughts? Or are your ears attune to hear the Spirit of God speaking to you? Make it an act of your will to keep your ears open to what God is saying to you through His Word and the Holy Spirit speaking to your heart.

I don't want to miss what God is saying to me—do you? Proverbs 1:33 says, *"Whoso hearkeneth unto me shall dwell safely, and shall be quiet from fear of evil."* As we face uncertain days in the future, we will walk in safety and confidence as we trust in the Lord and listen carefully to what He tells us to do. *Nancy*

Impacting Generations

We are wrong if we think that our influence is only within the walls of our home! One eternal day we shall see how far reaching our mothering is! We will know that we trained our children for the Kingdom, and thereby also, their children, their children's children, and their children's grandchildren, and as many generations of great-grandchildren as come upon the earth! Generations of children are influenced by our being faithful to our mothering career! Mothers equal impressive generational impact. *Michelle*

- February 4 -

Ear Trainers

What is the first thing you teach children? To listen! You must teach them to listen attentively before they can obey. Speak eye-to-eye when you give orders so you will know your child has heard what you have asked. You can then expect immediate action. As they learn to listen, they will learn to obey. As they learn to obey you, they will learn to obey God.

They must also learn that delayed obedience is disobedience. What kind of ears are you training your children to have? Dull... lazy... defiant... resistant... gullible ears? Or are you teaching them to have *"swift"* ears, as we read in James 1:19? Dear mother, you determine the kind of ears your children have which will set them on a pattern for life! What kind of ears are you training today? *Nancy*

Keep Me Humble, Lord

When I lose patience or let daily frustrations spoil the gentleness and grace of my speech, I am quickly brought low and reminded of my need for growth. These struggles reveal my weaknesses and keep me humble!

> *"The LORD lifteth up the meek."* (Psalm 147:6)
> *"To set up on high those that be low."* (Job 5:11)
> *"God resisteth the proud, but giveth grace unto the humble."* (James 4:6)

Praise God for these reminders of how desperately we need Him and His wonderful promises. *Michelle*

My Greatest Joy

What is your greatest joy? III John 4 says, *"I have no greater joy than to hear that my children walk in truth."* Is this your greatest joy and longing? Not pursuing your own agenda, not getting a bigger house, not aiming for the best college for your children, but earnestly longing that they will walk in God's truth.

If this is your greatest joy, you will give your time, and order your household to make it happen. It won't automatically happen. It takes your WHOLE LIFE to ensure that your children walk in truth, especially in the midst of this deceived world.

I look out the window and see about eight of our grandchildren playing football on the lawn. What a blessing to see them growing tall and strong physically, but my greatest joy is to see them growing tall and strong in the Lord. *Nancy*

Your Mission Field

I love to hear missionary stories of life on the field overseas. However, I also love to hear missionary stories of life on the home front. We are all missionaries, and we are all on the field! Some of us are paid by an organization to be missionaries, and some of us are missionaries as parents and mentors. Both are works worthy of commendation and recognition. One is not higher than the other.

How is the harvest going in your mission field? *Michelle*

- February 6 -

Yield to the Spirit

My inherent personality is to organize and tell everyone what to do in every situation. It's a good trait to make things happen and get things done, but not necessarily a good trait to bring the peace and sweetness of the Lord into the home. I have to cultivate a continual yielded spirit to the Lord.

We daily face moments and situations where we can either "have it our way" or yield to the Lord. Let's get into the habit of constantly saying, "I yield to you, Holy Spirit."

As it becomes the habit of your life to yield to the Lord in every situation, it will become easier to yield to your husband, too. The words of Jesus are true that the burden of life becomes easy when we yield to the yoke, rather than resisting it (Matthew 11:28-30). *Nancy*

Continuing Debt

I love this Scripture in Romans 13:8 NIV, *"Let no debt remain outstanding, except the continuing debt to love one another, for he who loves his fellowman has fulfilled the law."* Loving each other is a "continuing debt," one we will forever owe. Let's work on it by loving truly and deeply today.

Love like there's no tomorrow, and today will be amazing! *Michelle*

A Yielded Life

"Neither yield ye your members as instruments of unrighteousness unto sin: but yield yourselves unto God... and your members as instruments of righteousness unto God" (Romans 6:13).

I yield my ears, Lord, to listen to your voice.
I yield my eyes, Lord, to see situations as you see them.
I yield my tongue, Lord, to speak life-giving words to my family.
I yield my heart, Lord, to obey your Word.
I yield my hands, Lord, to work joyfully in my home.
I yield my womb, Lord, to your sovereignty.
I yield my feet, Lord, to serve you in my home. Amen.

Nancy

Rejoicing Will Come

In Matthew 18:10-14 ESV we read about the Father's deep concern over one lost sheep. *"He rejoices over it more than over the ninety-nine that never went astray."* A parent's heart can hardly bear it if one of the flock goes astray. They may even face condemnation from others, yet the Father rejoices *"more"* over the return of the lost sheep than over the 99 that never strayed.

Take heart and keep praying! Rejoicing will come! *Michelle*

Blessings of Fearing the Lord

Psalm 147:11-14 says, *"The Lord taketh pleasure in them that FEAR HIM, in those that hope in His mercy."* Oh the blessings of walking in the fear of the Lord.

When you walk in the fear of the Lord, God says He will strengthen the bars of your gates, He will bless your children within you, He will give you peace in your home, and He will fill you with the finest of wheat!

Let's not be deceived—the fear of the Lord results in blessings; the fear of man brings a snare! May God help us to walk in His fear, rather than in the fear of man. *Nancy*

Don't Take Love for Granted

Does someone in your life love you? As a believer, you already have the love of the Father, His son, Jesus Christ, and the promise of eternal life to look forward to. Today, you also enjoy the love and affection of one or two or more people. You are richly blessed. Give your loved ones a hug and kiss today, and show your thankfulness. Revel in your blessings. *Michelle*

- February 9 -

Don't Be Disappointed

Do you feel that no one wants to listen to the understanding God has given you about having children or other precious truths God has revealed to you? Don't be disappointed. In II Chronicles 30:10-11 NASB we read, *"The couriers passed from city to city... but they laughed them to scorn, and mocked them. Nevertheless, some men... humbled themselves and came to Jerusalem."*

We don't stop sharing truth just because people ridicule the truth. We keep on testifying with sweetness in our spirit and a smile on our face. As we are faithful to continually drop seeds of truth, there will be those who humble themselves and receive the truth. We sow the seed; God does the watering. *Nancy*

Overlook Insults

We are often quick to show our annoyance, especially in the comfort of our home! It is so easy to express immediate annoyance to our husband or children when they do something that irritates or insults us, isn't it?

I was deeply challenged today by Proverbs 12:16 NIV: *"A fool shows his annoyance at once, but a prudent man overlooks an insult."* Only fools show their annoyance immediately! Only fools cannot overlook insults. Only fools complain about them. I certainly do not want to be a fool when this Proverb teaches me how to be prudent. *Michelle*

- February 10 -

Cheer Up

John 16:33 says, *"In the world ye shall have tribulation: but be of good cheer; I have overcome the world."* Are you finding the pressures of daily life getting on top of you? Cheer up!

Because Jesus lives in a state of rest, you can live in rest, too, as you abide in Him. In Christ, there is a place of rest, even when life is overwhelming. I prove this daily. Are you suffering trials and sorrows? We can't seem to avoid them in this life, can we? Cheer up! Take courage. God understands and is with you in every trial and sorrow.

There is nothing that Jesus has not overcome, and because He lives in you, you will overcome also! What does the hymn say? "Overcoming daily with the Spirit's sword, Standing on the promises of God." You might like to sing this hymn at Family Devotions this evening. *Nancy*

More than Coffee!

Psalm 68:35 says, *"The God of Israel is He that giveth strength and power unto His people."* Isaiah 40:29 is another wonderful promise to tired mothers: *"He giveth power to the faint; and to them that have no might He increaseth strength."*

What incredible truths to stand upon. No need to feel downtrodden or zapped. Some folks only have coffee to lift them up! We have the God who gives power and strength to the weak! *Michelle*

- February 11 -

World-Changing Ministry

Would you love to be involved in a world-changing ministry? Do you want to feel useful and do something that impacts society? I want to encourage you, mother, that when you embrace your calling of motherhood to receive the babies God chooses to give you, when you raise them to contend for the faith and to stand undaunted against the enemy, that you are involved in a world-influencing ministry!

The greatest threat to the progressives and socialists are strong godly families who are raising children who will stand unflinchingly against the devil's deceptions. They are a force to be reckoned with. You will face disappointments and challenges, but never give up! The cost is too great. *Nancy*

Good Principles

It can be very easy to feel disappointment and focus on unmet needs. Look at Christ. He had no place to call His own (Luke 9:58). His loved ones let Him down (Matthew 26:40). The cost of the impending cross was overwhelming (Mark 14:36).

What were His coping strategies? Jesus prayed. He obeyed the will of the Father and offered Himself as a servant to others. When He rebuked, He did so in love, without any planks to remove from His own eye. These are good rules to live by. *Michelle*

- February 12 -

A Good Day

At the end of each creating day, God stated, *"It is good!"* Wouldn't it be great to say at the end of your day, "It's been a good day"? Maybe you don't always think your days are good days! You feel overwhelmed and wonder what you are accomplishing. Dear mother, God's Word tells you that "loving your husband, loving your children, and keeping the home, etc." are "good" things.

If you say and do something loving to your husband today, it is a GOOD DAY! If you manage to do your laundry, dishes, and prepare nutritious meals for your family, it is a GOOD DAY. If you nurse your baby and spend time loving your children and reading to them, it is GOOD DAY!

When your husband arrives home this evening, instead of groaning about all the problems, confess, "It's been a GOOD day, Darling." *Nancy*

More Kisses

My husband says I need to post on how to love your husband more! Hmm! I guess I need to give him more cuddles, more kisses, more hugs, more snuggles, more loving touches, more smiles, more eye contact, and more conversation. I need to spend more time pondering how to make his life better since that is one of my primary goals as his wife.

Now you know what I am up to this week. How about you? *Michelle*

Keep Trusting

The psalmist cried out, *"I trusted on, even while I said, 'Great is my distress!'"* (Psalm 116:10 Fides). Even in great distress, the psalmist continued to trust the Lord. Often we can start out trusting, but when the difficulty or affliction doesn't go away, or it just gets too hard, we stop trusting. May God help us to keep *"trusting on."* It's an ongoing trust! I am always encouraged by the following lines:

> *Trust Him when dark doubts assail thee,*
> *Trust Him when thy strength is small,*
> *Trust Him when to simply trust Him*
> *Seems the hardest thing of all.*
>
> *Trust Him, He is ever faithful;*
> *Trust Him, for His will is best;*
> *Trust Him, for the heart of Jesus*
> *Is the only place of rest.*

Nancy

The Grand Trickle

I think it is amazing that all the energy we pour out for our family now is going to trickle down and have huge impacts on our grandchildren and great-grandchildren. That makes our daily effort so much more meaningful, doesn't it? *Michelle*

- February 14 -

A Soft Heart

How do you keep your marriage together? Keep your heart soft! Jesus told the Pharisees in Matthew 19:8-9 NASB, *"Because of your hardness of heart Moses permitted you to divorce your wives; but from the beginning it has not been this way."*

Jesus exposed that a marriage falls apart when we allow our heart to get hard. Are you hardening your heart against your husband in some area? Are you being stubborn and obstinate? Get on your knees and ask the Lord to give you a soft heart before your marriage deteriorates.

If you let Him, the Holy Spirit will work this grace in your heart. You will not only save your marriage, but also save the generations to come from hurt and heartache. *Nancy*

Treasure Your Sweet Husband

Are you enjoying Valentine's Day? We all know that we don't "need" a day to celebrate our husband, but it is special to have a day to focus on the beauty of love. Treasure your sweetie today. If you don't have a sweetie, and you long for one, use today to pray toward that end. To have a mate to share your life with is a very precious gift. *Michelle*

- February 15 -

The Best Qualification

What degree do you have after your name? B.A.? M.Sc.? What degrees are you encouraging your children to go after? Can I guide you into the most important of all?

Have you heard of A.U.G.? It's the one I studied for as a young person. In fact, I'm still working on it, can you believe it? It's found in II Timothy 2:15, *"STUDY to shew thyself APPROVED UNTO GOD (A.U.G.), a workman that needeth not to be ashamed, rightly (or accurately) dividing the word of truth."*

You can study for this degree together as a family. It will set you and your family on a path of success. Joshua 1:8 says, *"This book of the law shall not depart out of thy mouth; but thou shalt meditate therein day and night, that thou mayest observe to do according to all that is written therein: for then thou shalt make thy way prosperous, and then thou shalt have good success."* Nancy

Affirm Your Blessings

Remember the power of affirmations. Confess how much you love your God, your life, your husband, and your children. After that, the little or large annoyances in life are put in their proper place where they belong—low on the totem pole. *Michelle*

- February 16 -

The Power of Silence

When Jesus was unjustly accused, *"He kept silent... He did not answer with regard to even a single charge"* (Matthew 26:63 and 27:12-14 NASB). Yet, how easily we react when someone accuses us or does not say the right thing to us! How easily we retort back to our husband whom we are meant to honor!

May God help us to keep soft, sweet, or silent in the face of accusation. *Nancy*

Slow to Speak

I have been learning ever so gradually the beauty of those three little words, *"Slow to speak"* (James 1:19). Oh, the pain and folly that could be avoided if I would pause and think more before I speak! Added to that, the extra time it would give me to listen and digest what was said to me!

These three little words are certainly worth remembering. *Michelle*

- February 17 -

Face the Challenge

"Do not fear or be dismayed, tomorrow GO OUT TO FACE THEM, FOR THE LORD IS WITH YOU" (II Chronicles 20:15-17 NASB).

Is there some situation you are dreading to face? Perhaps fear is overtaking you. The mountain looks too big. Dear mother, you can face it! Not in your own strength, but because GOD IS WITH YOU!

He will anoint you. He will help you. He will give you strength beyond your own! Put your trust in the Lord and face the situation. *Nancy*

Greater Than Your Woes

How are you today? Standing in a storm, or basking in the sun? We all face both, since this side of heaven has trials. May we find our joy, comfort, peace, and strength in Him who is greater than all our woes and blesses us beyond measure. Smile. Know how precious and loved you are, and the amazing heritage you are leaving by living your life for Him. *Michelle*

- February 18 -

Sacred Work

You would think it would be a holy task to be a priest, wouldn't you? Do you want to know some of their holy tasks? They had to take charge of the utensils... look after the furniture... the flour, wine, and oil... mix the spices... bake bread every week... and take responsibility over the things baked in pans (1 Chronicles 9:28-32).

"But these are menial tasks," you say. Yes, the priests were "set apart" by God for these appointed tasks.

You are also set apart by God to take charge of your kitchen, cook meals, bake bread and care for your family. It is sacred work, especially when you do it unto the Lord! *Nancy*

Never Heard a Regret

Mark Twain said, "Twenty years from now you will be more disappointed by the things that you didn't do than by the ones you did do. So throw off the bowlines. Sail away from the safe harbor." This applies to family planning. What appears like sailing away from the "safe harbor" of your control is actually a peace-filled journey.

Regret is often expressed when fertility has been limited, but I've never heard regret from those who trusted God for children, regardless of the number of children He gave them. *Michelle*

- February 19 -

Receive the Word

Do you read God's Word and not get anything out of it? Do you hear preaching and yet not get anything? We have to do more than read and listen. We have to RECEIVE! James 1:21 says, *"Receive with meekness the engrafted word, which is able to save your souls."* The New American Standard Bible says, *"In humility receive the word implanted which is able to save your souls."*

When you open God's Word, get into the mode of RECEIVING, even when you don't like what it is saying! When a baby is conceived, if it doesn't implant, it will die. If the Word is not IMPLANTED into our lives, it will be ineffective. As you read the Word, respond with, "Yes, Lord, I receive this rebuke." "Yes, Lord, thank you for this promise." "Yes, Lord, I will obey your Word."

Let the Word implant! Teach your children how to RECEIVE God's Word into their lives, too, for this is when it has the power to save their souls. *Nancy*

Welcome Home

As I made a purchase at our local cheese factory today, I watched a middle-aged husband and father finish his shift. As I left the building, I saw him literally run to his car in such a hurry to get home to his wife and children. It put a smile on my face as I wondered how often my husband races to get home to us. Do I disappoint his hopeful anticipation when he arrives or do I reinforce it? *Michelle*

- February 20 -

Refreshed and Revived

Are you going through trouble and difficulty? Does everything seem on top of you? In Psalm 138:7 David confesses, *"Though I walk in the midst of trouble, Thou wilt revive me"* (Psalm 138:7). God doesn't say that you won't go through trials, but He promises that He will revive you in the midst of them.

The word "revive" is *chayah* and means "to live anew, to recover, refresh, rebuild." Take your eyes off your trial and lift your heart to the Lord. In the midst of your trouble God will revive and rebuild you!
Nancy

Jesus Understands

Are you feeling tired, faced with constant demands and barely time to eat or lay your head down to rest? Are you surrounded by people and dealing with one thing after another? Does everyone need you at the same time?

You are living as Jesus did. He had no place to lay His head. He finally caught some shuteye on the boat, only to be woken up to deal with a crisis. When He disembarked, He dealt with another crisis (Matthew 8:18-34).

He knows what you are going through. He is interceding for you.
Michelle

- February 21 -

Guard on All Sides

Dear mother, you are the watchdog of your home. Don't give up your watch! God appointed gate-keeping watchers over His tabernacle at the entrance and on all four sides! They also watched over the sacred tent all night (I Chronicles 9:17-27).

The Proverbs 31 woman who *"looks well to the ways of her household"* is also a watchwoman! The phrase, "looks well" is the same Hebrew word that is used for a *"watchman unto the house of Israel"* (Ezekiel 33:7).

Don't let the deceiving enemy into your home. Watch your entrance and guard your home ON ALL FOUR SIDES! *Nancy*

A New Creation

If you have negative thoughts and constantly tell yourself you're not capable, you'll give up. How much more do we, as believers, have the right tools to be positive? We have the power of the Spirit of God living in us. We are a new creation. We should never give up! *Michelle*

- February 22 -

Shake the World!

"The neighbor sees a freckled-faced, short-nosed boy, but the mother sees only a face of beauty, and out of its eye looks a man who is going to help shape and maybe shake the world." I like this quote, don't you?

Don't despair if your child or children are not yet all you dream they will be. It takes effort, prayer, time, and years to raise a mighty son or daughter for God. Did you know that the Levites were not considered ready to work in the house of the Lord until they were 20 years old? (I Chronicles 23:24-27).

The more difficult your child, the more you will pray. The extra prayers will eventuate in extra blessings. When I was a child my uncles called me "the devil incorporated!" But my parents didn't give up. They prayed. My grandparents prayed. And God answered! *Nancy*

Take Heed

I must confess that I've been spending too much time playing the "What if?" game—fretting over circumstances that may never come to pass and that I have no control over anyway! At Family Devotions we read, *"Take heed to yourselves, lest your hearts be weighed down... with cares of this life, and that Day come on you unexpectedly"* (Luke 21:34). I was convicted! Do I want to be found in such a state on that Day? No way! I need to rest in Him and relax. How about you? *Michelle*

- February 23 -

Memorize

Recently, a young man (18 years old) stayed with us for a night as he traveled to his destination. What a joy to see a young man with his face set to do the will of God. More than that—a young man who loves to memorize God's Word. He has memorized 12 books of the Bible so far, including longer books such as Luke, John, Romans, and Hebrews!

He not only memorizes them in his mind, but keeps learning until he can recite them as though he was preaching them. He reminds me of my father who was still memorizing and preaching chapters of the Bible at 90 years of age!

What Scripture are you memorizing with your children this week? Romans 10:9-10 are important Scriptures for your children to memorize. You could start on these if you haven't already learnt them. *Nancy*

God's Creation is Perfect

I had a revelation today. For the first time in my life, I thanked God for making me "me." I have thanked Him for seemingly everything else— the privilege of being a mother, a wife, a believer, health, safety, family, friends, and provisions, but not for how He created me, just who I am (Psalm 139:13-18). Have you thanked God for the way He created "you"? *Michelle*

- February 24 -

God is Never Weary

Isaiah 40:28 asks the question, *"Hast thou not known? Hast thou not heard, that the everlasting God, the LORD, the Creator of the ends of the earth, fainteth not, neither is weary?"*

Because we are finite, we get weary. However, our God is never weary. He will refresh your weariness. When you fall, His everlasting arms are underneath to gird you. When you are weak, and even fainting, He is your Strength.

Our God *"neither slumbers or sleeps"* (Psalm 121:3-5). He will even strengthen you while you sleep. He will take care of your problems while you sleep. He will guard you while you sleep. Trust in His unfailing love. *Nancy*

The Best Occupation

Some occupations leave people feeling unappreciated and unrecognized, yet they dedicate so much of their time to it. We don't have that problem. We have a job that offers eternal recognition and the appreciation shows through the eyes of those that love us.

"Thank you, Lord, for the best occupation on earth!" *Michelle*

- February 25 -

Know Your Enemy

Be on the alert for the strategies of the enemy. The leftists are not interested in having children (perhaps one or two), but they know the power of children. They know they are the future destiny of the nation. Therefore, they cunningly capture the children of Christian parents.

How do they do this? It's easy. They make sure they are enlisted in the state education system (even pre-school) where they subtly indoctrinate them in socialist ideologies.

The nation cannot turn back to God and conservative values while Christian parents leave their children to be exploited by the enemy (Matthew 24:43). *Nancy*

Be Flexible

A hard lesson I have had to learn as a homeschool mother is to "leave room for life." I would set my agenda and then be flustered when "life" interfered and prevented me from accomplishing my daily goals. This made it difficult for me to have a good outlook and attitude.

I eventually learned the high value of "flexibility" as a character quality. The atmosphere in our home is much less stressful now. Leave room for life, and roll with the surprises in your day/week/year. *Michelle*

- February 26 -

Push Back the Darkness

As I lay awake in the early hours this morning, I felt God speaking to me about the state of God's people today—including me, of course. We have so little influence on the world because we are so much like the world! Many want to be more like the world than they want to be like Christ!

If we are going to affect the world for God, we will hate evil and love righteousness. We will stand for truth, no matter what the cost. We will turn away from the flesh and walk in the spirit. And we will pray.

Are we pushing back the darkness or being enveloped in the darkness? *"Have no fellowship with the unfruitful works of darkness, **but rather reprove them"** (Ephesians 5:11). Nancy*

God is in Control

I love how life continuously shows us that most of it is completely out of our control. It is such a great comfort knowing that our heavenly Father is very much in control. Just like a small child, I can leave all my concerns with Him and rest in His loving sovereignty.

This is such a peaceful thought, and I find myself dwelling on it often. We are richly blessed to have this comfort, especially when life throws us its curve balls. *Michelle*

- February 27 -

Establish God's Kingdom

You are pregnant! But you are scared to tell your parents or parents-in-law! You know you'll get a negative reaction (or maybe even a violent reaction)! May I encourage you that you only have to get through the next few months? When your precious baby is born, their hearts will change. No one can resist a baby!

Your parents and friends have this negative reaction because they have been conditioned to respond this way. Society, the media, and the education system all teach that you shouldn't have too many babies. Instead, they want you to give your life to a career or a job that you will leave behind and which will have little impact on the nation or on eternity! Their minds have been conditioned to believe lies from Satan who hates life.

But don't lose heart. They'll love your baby when he or she comes! Every new baby is a revelation of God's truth and God's kingdom, which is a kingdom of life. You are helping to establish the kingdom of God on earth and in heaven. *Nancy*

Mommy Time

Motherhood is more than a fulltime job. It is the best and most fulfilling way we spend our time. But, it can be exhausting and draining at times; and therefore, I quote my DVD exercise trainer, "If you NEED a break, take a break. But don't take a break because you WANT one. Take one if you NEED one and then come back as soon as you are able." No shame in needing a little "Mommy time." Then come back to your nation-impacting career. *Michelle*

Heavenly Practical

Can you be heavenly practical? The Bible informs us we can.

Philippians 3:20 tells us that our manner of life is in heaven! In other words, the life we live in our homes, our down-to-earth life of washing dishes, doing laundry, cleaning, changing diapers, and caring for our family should be a heavenly life.

As we allow the life of Jesus to live through us, we will experience a life filled with love, joy, peace, and gentleness, even in the midst of our practical mundane chores.

May heaven fill your home today. *Nancy*

God's Timing is Perfect

As a mother of eleven, I must say that I take tremendous peace in knowing that God has spaced each one of our children, including the six we lost. Whether they are 14 months or 34 months apart, the Lord's timing is always perfect.

I am thankful we left it all with the Lord. We don't have to look back and question whether we made the right "timing" decisions. This is another small mercy when we leave the Lord in control of our fertility. *Michelle*

- February 29 -

A Gentle Spirit

"Let your gentle spirit be known to all men" (Philippians 4:5 NASB). Gentleness is one of the fruit of the Spirit, one that's easy to show to folk you meet outside the home. But what about those within your home?

Do you have a gentle spirit toward your husband? Are your words gentle? Do you manifest a gentle spirit as you deal with your children? This is a challenge, isn't it? We can't do it in our own flesh; only by the life of Jesus living through us.

"Dear Father, please anoint me with your spirit of gentleness today. Let everyone around me in my home be encompassed with it. Amen." *Nancy*

Never Too Late

Are you having one of those days that is filled with constant strife? Perhaps the children are not behaving well, or maybe your marriage relationship is strained and you're not getting along?

You can turn things around! It is never too late to redeem the day. We serve a God of Redemption. He will bless all of your efforts to turn the tide, make changes, and restore peace and joy. Step out and make the change. *Michelle*

- March 1 -

Renew My Mind, Lord

God does not want us to stay in the rut of our old fleshly way of thinking. He wants to lead us on to His ways and thoughts. Ephesians 4:23 says, *"Be renewed in the spirit of your mind."* To be renewed comes from two Greek words, *ana* meaning "again" and *neos* meaning "to renew, make young, renovate."

We have to be renewed **again and again**! Each new day! Way's Translation reads, *"You must pass through a **process of renewal** by the Spirit dwelling in your mind."* It doesn't only mean to change your opinion (because you can change your opinion continually), but it means to allow the Holy Spirit to renew the *spirit* of your mind which will change the course of your life! *Nancy*

Live Today Like It's Your Last

Psalm 90:12 says, *"Teach us to number our days, that we may apply our hearts unto wisdom."* When the brevity of life is at the forefront of our mind, our priorities will instantly fall into place. We will focus on the truly important things, and our attitudes will be right.

Do you want a heart of wisdom? Live as though this day may be your last, or someone else's last; and treat everyone accordingly. *"Let us consider one another to provoke unto love and to good works"* (Hebrews 10:24). *Michelle*

- March 2 -

Fresh and New

God's renewing in our minds is always fresh, new, and youthful. He leads us out of the old and stuffy into new life in Christ! Leave the rut of your old way and be open to God's way.

Pray with me, "Father, please expose every worldly and humanistic thought pattern that is entrenched in my mind and all the old man-made traditions that hold me in bondage. Save me from being stubborn in my thought patterns. I yield my mind and heart to you. Please renew me daily by the power of your Holy Spirit and the power of your living Word. In the name of Jesus. Amen."

I am always challenged by Romans 12:2 in the J. B. Phillips' translation, *"Don't let the world around you squeeze you into its mould, but let God re-mould your minds from within." Nancy*

No Excuses!

"I don't have time," "It won't work," or "It's just too hard!" These statements translate to me as, "I don't want it badly enough," "It's not important enough to me," "I'm not motivated enough to bother," or "I'm too afraid to step out of my comfort zone."

No more excuses! Be radical. Be the life-giving energy and excitement in your home. Be so full of life that you are a magnet that others can't help but want to be around. *Michelle*

- March 3 -

A God-Fashioned Life

Paraphrasing Ephesians 4:22-23 into modern day English, I don't think I could say it better than Eugene Peterson: *"Everything—and I do mean everything—connected with that old way of life has to go. It's rotten through and through. GET RID OF IT! And then take on an entirely new way of life—a God-fashioned life, a life renewed from the inside and working itself into your conduct as God accurately reproduces His character in you."*

May the life of Jesus so permeate our lives that it will flow through every member of our body and overflow into everything we do in our home, even the most mundane chore. *Nancy*

No Doof!

One of the harder, yet healthier ways to live counter-culture is to stay away from "doof!" Doof is food spelled backwards, and it is a poor substitute for real, God-created food that nourishes and builds up.

Let's feed our families food and not doof! *Michelle*

- March 4 -

A Place of Refuge

Is your home a refuge? Is it a refuge from evil and the storms of life? Proverbs 14:26 tells us that parents who fear the Lord will make their home a *"place of refuge."* It is the same Hebrew word that speaks of God as our refuge, the One to whom we run for protection.

As we walk in the fear of the Lord each day, we will seek to keep evil from our home. We will speak peace to storms that arise, for our home is a shelter where we hide from the wild tempests outside.

We won't send our children out into the world to be educated, where they will be subtly brainwashed in humanism and socialism. We will protect them in our *"home of refuge"* while we make them strong. When they are mature and ready, we will send them forth to face the challenges of life. *Nancy*

Be Realistic!

I feel great on the days my "To Do" list is accomplished, but these are not the best days in our home. For us, an amazing and memorable day is where the family enjoys each other's company with laughter and sharing. If the list gets completed in the midst of enjoying one another's company, that's a bonus.

A list that causes strife and stress is likely an unrealistic list. *Michelle*

- March 5 -

As in God's Home, So in My Home

Jesus told us to pray, *"As in heaven, so in earth"* (Luke 11:2). Lift your vision higher today, dear mother. God wants His will to be accomplished in your home, just as in His heavenly home.

He wants the atmosphere of heaven to be the atmosphere of your home. As He fills heaven, He wants to fill your home with His presence. Will you let Him?

Think on this truth and confess it out loud over and over again today, *"As in heaven, so in earth."*

Now make it a little more personal, *"As in God's home, so in my home!" Nancy*

Good Ole Days

Two-year-old Solana is getting into all kinds of mess with her sister's flour. Enjoy these moments and don't let the mess get to you. You are making memories to last a lifetime. Our children fondly remember the times when things happen that shouldn't happen. Remember, these are the good ole days! *Michelle*

- March 6 -

God is My Sanctuary

Do you feel lonely, out of sorts, full of fears, or down in the dumps? You don't have to stay in this state! Did you know there is a sanctuary where you can run? It is God Himself! He is your refuge and hiding place, and He waits for you to run to Him. As you run into His heart, you will find safety, comfort, help, and deliverance.

Ezekiel 11:16 says, *"Although I have cast them far off among the heathen... yet will I be to them as a little SANCTUARY."* No matter what your situation, God is always our SANCTUARY (which is the same word that is used for the tabernacle and the temple where God dwelt in all His Shekinah glory).

Don't stay in your depressed state one minute longer! Run into God! Hurry! *Nancy*

Love Begets Love

I read the quote, "Sometimes you have to watch someone love something before you can love it yourself. It's as if they are showing you the way."

I think it is true on many levels, but also motherhood. When others see you truly loving motherhood, their hearts are often moved to love it, too! Even your own husband's heart can be moved to embrace children when he sees the joy and love you have for your children. *Michelle*

- March 7 -

Seven Necessary Questions

As I honestly seek to answer these questions about my actions towards my husband, would you like to also?

Am I **N**ourishing my husband with love?
Am I **N**urturing him and ministering to his needs—physically, emotionally and spiritually?
Am I being **N**ice to him, or just plain grouchy?
Am I **N**oticing him and giving him time in my busy schedule?
Am I **N**esting the home to provide him a place of solace?
Am I **N**obly revealing a picture of Christ, and His church, through my marriage?
Am I **N**ever giving up in my commitment to my marriage?

Nancy

Power of Faith

"Now faith is the substance of things hoped for, the evidence of things not seen" (Hebrews 11:1).

I need this reminder today in my sleep-deprived state. God will give me strength to be pleasant, sweet, and nurturing. His power through me will help me to build up and not tear down. There will be encouragement, smiles, and praise—not self-pity! *Michelle*

- March 8 -

Undisputed Ruler

"The blessed and only Potentate, the King of kings, and Lord of lords; who only hath immortality, dwelling in the light which no man can approach unto... to whom be honor and power everlasting" (I Timothy 6:15-16). As Potentate, God is Sovereign Lord, the undisputed and absolute Ruler!

But, I am challenged. Is He the undisputed Ruler of my life, of my possessions, of my womb, of my finances, of my children—in fact, of everything?

Who is the Potter and who is the clay in my life? What about in your life? *Nancy*

Our Children are Watching

Much of learning is caught more than taught. How do we react to annoyances, troubles, offensives, and anger? How are we speaking to and about others? What is our witness before our children? I pray, *"Set a watch, O Lord, before my mouth; keep the door of my lips"* (Psalm 141:3).

We must walk the walk and talk the talk, leaning daily on our only Hope of Success. *Michelle*

- March 9 -

Real Knowledge

Colossians 1:10 say, *"That ye might walk worthy of the Lord unto all pleasing, being fruitful in every good work, and increasing in the knowledge of God."*

Regarding *"the knowledge of God,"* the margin of my Bible notes, *"increasing in REAL KNOWLEDGE."* It is the knowledge of God that is real knowledge.

Fill your children with real knowledge, morning and evening as you have Family Devotions, and throughout the day in your daily activities (Deuteronomy 6:6-9 and Colossians 3:16). Remember that in Christ Jesus are *"hidden ALL the treasures of wisdom and knowledge"* (Colossians 2: 3). *Nancy*

Still Snuggling

My friend and I sat across from each other in a restaurant. I'll never forget a very elderly couple that came in with a painfully slow gait, holding hands and taking care as they prepared to sit. When they sat, they chose to sit on the same side of the bench, rather than across from each other. So sweet. They wanted to be close together to snuggle. May this be our testimony. *Michelle*

- March 10 -

Balance of Grace and Truth

John 1:14 tells us, *"And the Word was made flesh, and dwelt among us, (and we beheld His glory, the glory as of the only begotten of the Father) full of grace and truth."* What an amazing fact that Jesus Christ, the Son of God, became flesh and lived in this world. Even more amazing is that Jesus Christ still wants to become flesh and dwell in this world. He now dwells in His redeemed saints.

How did He reveal His glory? Jesus came *"full of grace and truth."* He wants to manifest His grace and truth through me. And through you—in your home, as you daily interact with your children. He wants us to be messengers of His truth, never compromising. But He also wants us to walk in grace, showing compassion and undeserving love, even when people do not accept the truth.

Dear Mother, ask God to show you how to walk in "grace and truth" as you train your children. Truth on its own can become legalistic; grace on its own becomes sloppy and does more harm to our children. Ask God to give you the balance and to work these graces in your life. This is what He wants to do for He dwells in you. *Nancy*

Heart Melting Moment

The highlights of motherhood are too numerous to list, but this one warmed my heart. My tiny one-and-a-half-year-old daughter came over to me with outstretched arms, and as I lifted her, she lay her head on my shoulder while uttering this for the very first time, "I love you!" What melts a Mama's heart faster than that? Completely unexpected and so very much appreciated! *Michelle*

71

- March 11 -

Flesh or Spirit?

Are you walking in the flesh or in the spirit? Whichever one you feed the most will rise up and rule!

You feed the flesh when you give into your feelings of anger and frustration. Starve it instead!

Feed the spirit, even though it is against everything you feel. Bite your tongue and say a kind word instead of a critical one. Express thankful words instead of complaining ones.

The Holy Spirit lives within you to enable you. Live the new life that is in you, not the old life of the flesh. *Nancy*

Life is Sweeter

Today, our house will be filled with extra children, and excitement, as we celebrate our son's birthday. It is so wonderful to bless someone and celebrate their life with them. Family and friends are such precious gifts. I think I will take a moment to celebrate all of my loved ones today. Life is sweeter because they are in it, and I want them to know it! *Michelle*

- March 12 -

A Hearing Heart

Did you know that when God told Solomon that He would give him whatever he wanted, he asked for *"a hearing heart"* (1 Kings 3:3-14). The Hebrew word is *shama* and means, "to hear with attention and obedience, to give undivided listening attention."

Ask God to give you a hearing heart to hear Him speaking to you. Ask God to give you a heart to hear what your husband is saying to you. Ask God to help you to hear the needs of your children, even their unspoken needs.

Become a listening family. Teach your children how to have a heart that is attentive to hear. It is the greatest gift they can take into life. *Nancy*

Antidote to Negativity

Hand sanitizers are everywhere to help us guard against illness, yet the catchiest thing I see spreading is negativity! Praise God that we have an eternal focus and are able to overcome. Our positivity oozes and permeates all around us simply because we walk in thankfulness for our salvation. Good thing, as it is the only antidote to the negativity that wants to swallow us whole! *Michelle*

- March 13 -

What a Privilege!

Perhaps you are sitting on your rocking chair and nursing your baby as you read this post. What a powerful work you are doing. You are not only nurturing and blessing your baby, you are not only preserving your own body, but you are revealing the character of God. What could be more beautiful and powerful?

We see God's nurturing heart in Isaiah 49:15, *"Can a woman forget her sucking child, that she should not have compassion (wombness) on the son of her womb? Yea, they may forget, yet will I not forget thee."* This powerful anointing of protection, love, and nurturing that pours from you while you nurse your baby comes from God. Only God's anointing is even stronger. A mother may forget, but God will never.

We see the same character in Jesus when He cried over Jerusalem. *"How often would I have gathered thy children together, even as a hen gathereth her chickens under her wings, and ye would not!"* (Matthew 23:37). Rejoice that you have the privilege of revealing God's character. *Nancy*

How Many Hugs?

How many hugs will you give today? Little else matters but people, right? So show them how much you love them and put on your smile! *Michelle*

- March 14 -

Never Stuck

"A good man is never stuck!" This is a quote from my dear father who is now with the Lord. Every time he faced a challenge or difficulty, he confessed these words and always found a way to fix the problem. I grew up with this quote, our children grew up with it, and now our grandchildren say it each time they face a problem. It is being passed down the generations! *Nancy*

Away with Whining

Mothers are the first to get annoyed with complaining and whining in our children. Yet, do the children hear us complaining and whining ourselves? Adults struggle with this just as much as children, and yet it is tolerated and socially acceptable if you are "of age." What does this speak of our faith, character, and attitude?

I think we should leave our complaints and whining at the throne of God, as He is the only One who can fix things anyway. We need to bite our tongue and verbalize more positively. This is a clear way to shine in this dark world.

God can handle our complaints, as well as our praise, but let our husband, children, neighbors, and friends hear only our praise! To dwell on the negative does us no good! *Michelle*

A Positive Attitude

It all depends on our attitude! My Uncle Eion (my father's oldest brother, now passed away) faced many challenges in his life. His beautiful big home burnt to the ground. He went bankrupt. He also got diabetes, which resulted in the amputation of first one leg and then the other! In the midst of all these trials, he would confess with a smile on his face, "I'm the luckiest man alive!"

What are you complaining about? *Nancy*

Say "Yes" More!

I have been pondering about making sure my "yes" is "yes" and my "no" is "no," and how important it is to keep my word.

I also realize that I say "no" plenty more than I need to, often without even thinking about why. Many times I say "no" out of my own selfishness or my own lack of motivation, not because it is the right answer!

I want my "yes" to be "yes" and my "no" to be "no," but I want to say "yes" as much as possible. I must stop saying "no" simply out of convenience, especially to my family. *Michelle*

- March 16 -

The Buck Stops with God

There was a time in my life when I wrestled with the truth of trusting God to give the children He wants to give to us. One night, I woke up with the following words filling my mind, "The perfect will of God for your life will never contradict God's existing commandments." That was my answer. That settled it forever.

In other words, if we feel God is calling us to do something that would cause us to stop having children, it's not God's plan, but our own idea! God never contradicts what He has established and stated in the very beginning (Genesis 1:27-28). *Nancy*

You are a Nation Builder

The other day my baby girl, Solana, got into the *Above Rubies* stock. She had at least 10 *"I am a Nation Builder"* wristbands covering her arms! What a great reminder. She will be a nation builder one day!

As we raise children, we are building nations and impacting generations. Sometimes we get caught in ruts and forget the impact we are making. Our task is huge, and our influence is far reaching!

You are a Nation Builder! It is massive and awe-inspiring! *Michelle*

- March 17 -

My Defining Glory

A beautiful mother shared with me that a woman commented to her, "Why is it so important for you to be pregnant?" She didn't know what to answer.

I suggested she reply, "Because this is my defining glory!"

God reveals to us in Hosea 9:11 that "conception, pregnancy, and birth" are the GLORY of the nation! What a privilege to walk in the glory God has given to us. *Nancy*

Why Grumble?

After being away, there are many tasks to catch up on at home. Many of the tasks are repetitive, such as tidying, laundry, dishes, and meal planning. I caught myself feeling overwhelmed. I was just about to start the grumbling process in my brain over the sheer volume of work, but then stopped.

Once again, the Lord reminded me that He hears the same pleas, the same requests for forgiveness, and sees the same behaviors, yet never tires of me.

I will continue my tasks with joy, not grumbling. Thank you, Lord. *Michelle*

- March 18 -

Home of Prayer

Does your home belong to God? Jesus said, *"My house shall be called the house of prayer"* (Isaiah 56:7; Matthew 21:13). Therefore, if we confess that our home belongs to God, it will be a house of prayer.

Do those who live around you know your home is a house of prayer? Does heaven know your home is a house of prayer? Does the devil know your home is a house of prayer?

You may not always remember, but the devil remembers the power of prayer and will do everything to stop you. Don't let him! You can impact nations as you pray together as a family. *Nancy*

I Want Control

Sometimes I feel like I have to have some control and power. Therefore, today, I am going to control my tongue. It will take conscious effort, continuously throughout each hour, but by God's grace, victory shall be mine. *Michelle*

- March 19 -

Joyful Home

Does joy fill your home? God says in Isaiah 56:7 that *"I will... make them JOYFUL in My house of prayer."* Making your home a house of prayer will not make it morbid. On the contrary, it will make it joyful. Homes of prayer are joyful homes. How much joy is filling your home? *Nancy*

You Can!

Philippians 4:13 says, *"I can do ALL things through Christ who strengthens me."* A well-known Scripture, but do you really believe it? Are you truly living it? It means that you can do all the things you currently think you cannot.

You CAN be a sweet and loving wife! You CAN be a patient, attentive mother! You CAN be the ray of sunshine on the cloudy day! You CAN be the motivation when everyone around you is low! You CAN be the inspiration and the energy in the face of trials! You CAN be the pillar of strength and prayer in trying times! You CAN be the one to implement healthy eating and fitness in the family! You CAN be the magnet to which everyone gravitates.

Why? Because Christ in you strengthens you to do all these good things. *Michelle*

- March 20 -

Do Something New Today

Proverbs 14:11 says, *"The tabernacle of the upright shall **flourish**."* The Hebrew word for "flourish" is *parach* and means "to break forth as a bud, to bloom, to extend the wings and fly, to spread forth abundantly."

Spring is here! It's time for new things to break forth. Why don't you do something new today?

Love your husband a little more passionately. Love your children more exuberantly. Think of something new to do at your family meal table this evening—something you've never done before. Think of a new idea to bring delight into your home. *Nancy*

No. 1 Priority

Just before I left for a recent plane flight, I thought to myself, "I am way too busy. All I have time for is prayer!" I had the privilege of praying for each one of my family members individually during the flight.

Prayer is the one thing you cannot squeeze out of your schedule. It is the best thing you can do today. Do it now, even while you are cooking and cleaning. *Michelle*

- March 21 -

Stand Against Evil

"Who will rise up for me against the evildoers? or who will stand up for me against the workers of iniquity?" (Psalm 94:16). Do you want to do great things for God, yet you feel stuck?

You can be one of God's warriors who rise up against the evildoers, even from your home. You can pray. You can write emails and send faxes. You can send petitions. You speak truth at every opportunity. You can train your children to be truth speakers.

Stand resolutely for truth and righteousness, starting in your home. Be a force against evil and an advocate for righteousness. *Nancy*

Combat the Lies

I heard these lyrics today: "All we have to do is take these lies and make them true." How true this is in our culture—making lies into truth!

Don't be on the defense when you are standing for truth. Be on the offense. Proclaim truth to combat the lies everywhere you go, especially regarding the truth about marriage and children. In your home, too. *Michelle*

- March 22 -

Return to Justice

"Judgment shall return unto righteousness" (Psalm 94:15). The word return is *shuv* and means "a movement back to the point of departure, to turn back."

It is time for us to turn back to God's righteousness and justice. It is time for the church to turn back. It is time for the nation to turn back— back to the truth of God's eternal Word, not our own ideas.

We must start in our home, asking God to give us His righteous judgment and discernment in every situation we face. *Nancy*

Opportunities, Not Burdens

John Newton wrote, "We can easily manage if we will only take, each day, the burden appointed to it. But the load will be too heavy for us if we carry yesterday's burden over again today, and then add the burden of the morrow before we are required to bear it."

I like this quote, except I try not to think of daily loads, no matter how heavy, as burdens. I prefer to think of them as opportunities in the grand adventure of life! *Michelle*

- March 23 -

Remind God of His Promises

"(God) chose Mount Zion which He loves... the Lord loves the gates of Zion" (Psalm 78:68 and 87:1-3, 5). If God loves Jerusalem, shouldn't we? And if we love Jerusalem, we'll be praying for its blessing and protection.

Isaiah 62:6-7 says, *"I have set watchmen upon thy walls, O Jerusalem, which shall never hold their peace day nor night: ye that make mention of the Lord, keep not silence, and give Him no rest, till He establish, and till He make Jerusalem a praise in the earth."*

Are you daily praying together as a family for Israel and Jerusalem? *Nancy*

Eternal Investment

Research has proven the benefits of the family meal table, especially for children. Each meal where the family all gathers to share food, conversation, and prayer are eternal investments into the lives of your children and impacts their well-being.

Take time to have wonderful family meal times. Never forget the high value of this seemingly ordinary task. *Michelle*

God Gives Liberally

"If any of you lack wisdom…" Wow! I sure need it. I am currently facing situations where man's wisdom is not sufficient. I need divine wisdom. Thanks be to God that He has promised to give His wisdom LIBERALLY when we ask Him (James 1:5-7).

Maybe you need God's wisdom today, too. What mother doesn't need it every moment? Don't trust in your own resources. Cry out to God, and He will generously give you His wisdom. *Nancy*

Thank Your Husband

Like me, do you look after your children each day at home? As I tidied a very untidy little girls' room, I realized that I have not thanked my husband recently for allowing me the privilege to be home!

I am blessed, thanks to my husband's hard effort. I schedule my day only around our family, and it is so fulfilling. I need to thank my husband. How about you? *Michelle*

- March 25 -

Use Your Weapons

II Corinthians 10:4-5 tells us that God has given us weapons to pull down strongholds. The NASB says, *"The weapons of our warfare are not of the flesh, but divinely powerful for the DESTRUCTION OF FORTRESSES."* Are you facing mountains that are like a fortress? Are you thinking there is no way you can face it, let alone pull it down?

It is true that it is impossible in your own strength, but God is with you. You have the weapon of prayer, the power of the blood of Jesus, and the word of your testimony (Revelation 12:10). Use your weapons. *Nancy*

Treasured and Special

Do you know that you are so special? God chose to reveal Himself to you to experience His love and to raise children for His glory. You are very treasured, and you are doing an amazing job! God knew you would, and that's why He placed you exactly where you are. Enjoy your life and your home. *Michelle*

Abundant Joy

Are you going through a "great ordeal?" When the Macedonian believers were going through great affliction, they overflowed with abundant joy!

Are you going through a time of financial crisis? When the Macedonian believers were going through "deep poverty," they overflowed with liberality! They gave beyond their ability. They gave themselves to the Lord, but also to the believers. They put us modern believers to shame, don't they?

Let's find encouragement in the fact that our life is hid with Christ in God. We can therefore overcome no matter what our circumstances or finances. (II Corinthians 8:2). *Nancy*

Softer and Wiser

Life comes fraught with trials, and few of us remain unscathed by them. However, we have the resources to carry us through! When we are in the depths, He carries us tenderly. Slowly, we grow. He molds us more into His image, and we come out softer and wiser at the other end. The love of Christ flows through us as we support others who are struggling. Don't despair in the hard times. *Michelle*

- March 27 -

Don't Lose Heart

I have been challenged by Paul's confession, *"We do not lose heart"* (II Corinthians 4:16). Paul said these words in the midst of going through *"afflictions, hardships, distresses, beatings, imprisonments, tumults, labors, sleeplessness, and hunger"* (II Corinthians 6:4-10; 11:23-29; and 12:10).

What are you going through? Perhaps a few sleepless nights. Maybe you are upset because of negative words that have been said to you. We know little of real persecution.

Come on, dear mother, let's toughen up a bit! DON'T LOSE HEART! Stand strong against the pressures of life. Stand strong for your convictions. God is with you in every situation. *Nancy*

A Tool of Blessing

"The tongue of the wise is health" (Proverbs 12:18). Everyone is interested in healthy living, but health also depends on words. They can change the course of a day and even the course of a life! Do you feel your words are not making much of a difference? Think again. Your tongue is a powerful tool of blessing to impart wisdom, grace, love, and health! Watch and wait for the results! *Michelle*

- March 28 -

Soul Rest

What kind of atmosphere are you creating in your home today? Your children will remember the atmosphere of your home more than anything else. Jesus calls us to find rest in Him in the midst of our burdens and heavy labor. It's not a rest of inactivity, but SOUL REST in the midst of the busyness of life. It is the absence of tension and strained relationships.

Answer Jesus' invitation in Matthew 11:28-30, *"Come unto Me, all ye that labor and are heavy laden, and I will give you rest. Take My yoke upon you, and learn of Me; for I am meek and lowly in heart: and ye shall find rest unto your souls. For My yoke is easy, and My burden is light."*

Yield to God's will, and you will find the rest God has made available to you (Hebrews 4:9). As you live in this place of rest, your home will become a restful place, too. *Nancy*

Joy is Contagious

"Rejoice evermore" (I Thessalonians 5:16). We all desire joy although it cannot be bought or sold. When we see joy, we want it, too. Joy is available to us regardless of our financial status or our life circumstances, and it speaks volumes to all around!

Live your life full of love for others and full of joy. This is possible or we wouldn't be told to do it. *Michelle*

- March 29 -

Answer Kindly

What do you do when someone slanders you or says nasty things behind your back? God wants you to bless and answer kindly! *"Being reviled, we bless; being persecuted, we suffer it: being defamed, we entreat"* (I Corinthians 4:12-13).

The New American Standard Bible encourages us to "conciliate." What a lovely word! It means to "win over, gain favor by friendly acts, reconcile, or bring to state of friendship." That's a challenge, isn't it?

You will not be popular as you stand against the tide of compromise and humanism. Stand for the truth, expect reviling and disdain, but react with love and conciliation! *Nancy*

Day of Miracles

Are you seeing God's amazing power in your daily life? While vacationing as a family, we had a dental emergency in a remote area. The Lord provided above and beyond what any of us could have even hoped for! Even if we had been in a thriving metropolis, we likely would not have received such outstanding care. It is still a day of miracles. *Michelle*

- March 30 -

No Regrets

I recently heard a young mother with a new baby share that she feels guilty for not rushing around everywhere like her friends, when all she wants to do is stay home and care for her baby and children! Of course she is doing the right thing! What does a mother accomplish by gadding about? Nothing! This mother is establishing a beautiful relationship with her baby and strengthening her marriage and home. One day she will look back and have no regrets.

Be faithful in your home today, dear mother. One day you will receive the reward promised in Matthew 25:21, *"Well done, thou good and faithful servant: thou hast been faithful over a few things, I will make thee ruler over many things: enter thou into the joy of thy lord."* Nancy

Run for the Prize

In I Corinthians 9:24, we are told to run the race in order to get the prize. This is definitely our life goal—to obtain the prize of eternal life. There are times when my other, lesser goals cloud my vision and I forget to enjoy the run. Let's take time to enjoy the run. We will only pass each leg of the run once. *Michelle*

- March 31 -

Penetrating the Conscience

"Therefore, knowing the fear of the Lord, we persuade men... and I hope that we are made manifest also in your consciences" (II Corinthians 5:11 NASB).

If I am walking in the fear of God, I will want to persuade my children and people around me of the truth of the gospel. It is not enough to mention it to them; I must persuade them! Perhaps persuasion will precede the moving of the Holy Spirit in their lives.

As parents, our lives should affect the consciences of our children, as well as all we come in contact with. This should be the effect of our lives—filled with light to expose darkness, filled with truth to expose deceptions, and filled with the Holy Spirit to penetrate the conscience. *Nancy*

On the Other Foot

One day I bitterly questioned why my husband wasn't doing certain things for me. Why wasn't he being affectionate? Why wasn't he connecting with me, or trying to spend time with me? My husband asked if I was doing those things for him! And guess what? I wasn't!

Instead of complaining, I needed to be acting! If you are like me, you are married to an imperfectly perfect man, but when you really stop to count his amazing ways, you feel richly blessed and maybe undeserving of him. How can you love your husband better today? *Michelle*

- April 1 -

Keep in His Presence

We need God's strength moment by moment, don't we? How are we strengthened? Ephesians 6:10 (Way translation) encourages us, *"Be ye strengthened in the Lord's presence."*

Keep in His presence, and you will experience His strength, even in your weakness. Look to Him instead of your own strength. *Nancy*

Don't Believe the Lie!

I grew up in a culture where being a "stay-at-home mom" gave the impression that the mother must be fairly uneducated and unable to do much else with her life; hence, she "just" stayed home. What a complete and utter falsehood!

Running a home smoothly, training children through all the stages of life, figuring out how to feed a growing family with nourishing and wholesome food, and being a godly wife take more skill than many professions. Stay-at-home mothers need to be experts in far more than one field. It takes endurance, perseverance, diligence, wisdom, passion, research, and so much more.

How can anyone believe that the profession of motherhood is for the weak-minded? Home-keeping mothers are among the most gifted and competent members of society. *Michelle*

- April 2 -

Language of Thanks

Ephesians 5:4 NASB commands, *"No filthiness and silly talk, or coarse jesting, which are not fitting, but rather giving of thanks."*

Thankfulness should be the predominant language in our home. Are you in the habit of thanking God, not only for the good things, but for the difficult situations?

Our thankfulness to the Lord will spill over to our family. Do you thank your husband for the little things he does for you? Do you thank him for choosing you to be his wife? Do you thank him for taking out the trash? Well, if he doesn't take out the trash, and you have to do it yourself, thank him for something else!

What about your children? Do you thank them when they do their chores? Do you tell them you are glad God gave them to you? Today, why don't you thank your husband and each one of your children for something specific, maybe something for which you have never thanked them before? Your thankfulness to your family members will spill over to others outside your home, too. Think of someone else you can thank, and give them a call! *Nancy*

Snuggling Day

My three year old could not get enough of me today! He was on my lap, at my side, or at my feet. What a beautiful season of motherhood. To be so needed and adored. Who cares if some things don't get done? We snuggled the day away! *Michelle*

- April 3 -

The Perfume of Christ

What kind of aromas fill your home? Sweet or bad smells? The flesh gives off sour, bitter, grumpy, and horrible smells, doesn't it? The kind of stench that makes everyone in the home feel bad and want to run!

But Christ in us is a sweet-smelling savor, and He wants us to exude His sweet aroma throughout the home. Most husbands love fragrant perfumes (well, my husband does), but more than perfumes, we should constantly wear the perfume of Christ in our lives.

I am always challenged by II Corinthians 2:14 (J. B. Phillip's translation), *"We should have about us the **unmistakable scent of Christ.**"* How are you smelling today? Are your husband and children avoiding you or running to you? *Nancy*

Still Courting

I am honored to have the anniversary ring that my granddad gave my grandma years ago. It is inscribed with the word "courtship." When he gave it to her, he told his bride that after 25 years, he still felt like they were courting!

I hope to give this ring to one of my children as they follow the courtship path into marriage. May they, like my grandparents, still feel like they are courting at the end of their lives. *Michelle*

- April 4 -

In Every Place

I wrote yesterday about how God wants us to be a "sweet aroma." Did you notice the word, "sweet"?

However, there is more to it. We are to be a "sweet" aroma in "*every place*" (II Corinthians 2:14-15). Every place includes our home!

It means in the midst of what we are doing—when children are making us crazy, when our husband is rubbing us the wrong way, and when we are doing mundane chores like changing dirty diapers! Are we still giving off a sweet aroma? *Nancy*

A Different Perspective

"Your house reminds me of my grandma's home. I feel at home here with the crumbs on the floor."

I didn't know whether to feel pleased or insulted by my guest's comment. When I relayed this story to a wiser mom, she said, "Just throw some crumbs on your head, and you'll fit right in!"

Sometimes I just need to have a different perspective and a sense of humor. Do you need to lighten up today? *Michelle*

- April 5 -

Rejoice Anyway

People do dumb things. They say the wrong thing. They say things about us, or to us, that hurt us. The longer I live the more I realize that life is not perfect! It doesn't go the way we want!

So what do we do? We acknowledge that life is not perfect, and rejoice anyway! Getting upset will not change anything. Instead, we bless those who hurt us. We laugh instead of getting upset. We keep plodding on, trusting in the Lord, and smiling in the face of trials. *Nancy*

Joy Busters!

- Focusing on other's shortcomings and ignoring my own!
- Feeling sorry for myself instead of counting my blessings!
- Letting my prayer life slack and not leaving all my burdens at His feet!
- Not taking care of myself properly (eating, sleeping, exercising) instead of giving my best!
- Complaining instead of being thankful!
- Believing lies instead of remembering who I really am in Christ!

Stay tuned for more. *Michelle*

- April 6 -

A Colony of Heaven

We read this morning at Family Devotions, *"Our conversation is in heaven"* (Philippians 3:20). It actually means that our **homeland** is in heaven, or we are **citizens** of heaven! Moffat translates it, *"We are a colony of heaven."*

What a difference this would make to our every word and action in our home if we truly realized that we were citizens of heaven! Make your home a colony of heaven rather than this world. *Nancy*

More Joy Busters!

- Comparing myself covetously to others instead of being content!
- Being contentious instead of being gracious!
- Serving self instead of others!
- Feeling victimized instead of walking in victory!
- Creating self-defeat with negative self-talk!
- Forgetting that God has equipped me for daily life and mothering.

Michelle

Say the Name of Jesus

Does your heart need cheering today? There is only one who can truly cheer you in the depths of your soul. His name is Jesus.

Are you feeding sad? Speak the name of Jesus. Are you feeling unloved? Say the name of Jesus out loud. Are you feeling hurt and ungrateful? Say, "Thank you, Jesus."

Say His name over and over again throughout this day. You cannot stay dismal when you speak His name. I love the words of the hymn...

> *Who can cheer the heart like Jesus*
> *By His presence all divine,*
> *True and tender, pure and precious,*
> *O, how blest to call Him mine.*
> *All that thrills my soul is Jesus,*
> *He is more than life to me,*
> *And the fairest of ten thousand*
> *In my blessed Lord I see.*

Nancy

A Captivated Audience

Guess what? You were handpicked by God to share your faith with a captivated audience—your children. You are doing a wonderful job of lovingly shaping the lives of your children. Keep up the great work!
Michelle

- April 8 -

Overwhelmingly Conquer

Are you in distress? Going through tribulation? It is not enough to separate you from God's love! In fact, God promises that even in these difficult times, you can OVERWHELMINGLY CONQUER!

We read in Romans 8:37 NASB, *"But in all these things we overwhelmingly conquer through Him who loved us."* You cannot do it in your own strength, of course, but through Christ who loves you!

Don't dwell on your trials, but trust in God. He is totally faithful. Not even famine, tribulation, distress, persecution, famine, peril, or anything you will face can keep you from God's love. *Nancy*

Tell Them Now!

I have no idea why it is so easy to focus on the negative, but I want to encourage you to bless your loved ones with positive affirmation today. Many times I "think" the good thoughts about others, but speak the bad.

Today, I will speak the good, and affirm each of my loved ones. Life is too short to let those words go unspoken. I have family and friends that I adore, and they need to know it. I am sure you do, too. *Michelle*

- April 9 -

Secret of Joy

"Let no man seek his own good, but that of his neighbor"
(I Corinthians 10:24 NASB).

I am reminded again that my life does not revolve around me! I am not to seek to please myself, but to serve and bless others. The amazing revelation is that this lifestyle leads to joy and victory in my personal life and in my home.

To revolve my life around myself leads to misery and boredom! To serve my family results in fulfillment and joy. (Also read Romans 15:2 and I Corinthians 9:19; 10:33; 13:5 and Philippians 2:3-4). *Nancy*

Be Nice to Yourself

Sometimes it is a struggle to get all the things accomplished that you hope to do in a day. I know that my expectation level is often not in sync with the reality of time constraints. Therefore, I want to congratulate you on an amazing job if you made supper today. Well done! Celebrate every level of accomplishment, not only the days you think you've accomplished your list. *Michelle*

- April 10 -

God's Tender Words

Are you are going through a wilderness? Take heart. God has promised that in the wilderness experience, He will speak tenderly to you. Hosea 2:14 MLB says, *"I will take her to the wilderness, and I will speak tenderly to her heart."* The word is emotive and means "from the very heart."

God will speak to you heart to heart, but you will have to listen quietly for His tender words. It's hard to hear God speaking when you are consumed with your problem rather than listening to Him. *Nancy*

Heart Change

Discipline is training, not only a tool for punishment. The goal is to teach and modify. The motive is to help the child internalize (make it their own) righteous behavior. We don't want them to be "sitting on the outside, but standing up on the inside."

What we really desire is their hearts to be changed, not just their behavior. Of course, we need God's divine assistance. *Michelle*

The Best Day of Your Life

Each morning after Family Devotions my husband says to everyone, "May this be the most amazing day you have ever lived!" Sometimes, he goes through the alphabet... a letter for each new morning. For example, "May you have the most anointed, amazing, astounding, abounding, abiding with Christ, adding to knowledge, adventurous, and awesome day of your life!"

Each one gets up from their seats ready to enjoy the best day of their lives! Would you like to try this in your home? *Nancy*

Reap in Due Season

"And let us not be weary in well doing: for in due season we shall reap, if we faint not. As we have therefore opportunity, let us do good unto all men, especially unto them who are of the household of faith" (Galatians 6:9-10). This is the perfect verse for me to start my day. How about you? *Michelle*

- April 12 -

Stop Resisting

"For who resists His will?" (Romans 9:19 NASB). Why do we fight against God? Why do we fight against our great calling of motherhood? Why do we fight against our husband?

It's not much use because we will never win. Don't you find that life is much easier when you allow God to work in you a soft, humble, repentant, and submissive spirit? It's the opposite to the flesh, but it's the way to joy and victory. *Nancy*

A Love Letter

Mother Teresa wrote, "I am a little pencil in the hand of a writing God who is sending a love letter to the world."

May the world see your love to your children and the children around you, and may they be astonished at how much you esteem them. May the Holy Spirit convict them to change their hearts toward children, too.

Never underestimate your witness to a watching world. *Michelle*

- April 13 -

Reign in Life

Romans 5:17 says we are to *"reign in life by one, Jesus Christ."* You do not have to wait until the millennium to reign with Christ. He wants you to reign in your daily life right now! In your kitchen. In whatever is happening in your home!

How do you reign? By not giving into the desires of the flesh such as anger, rebellion, and stubbornness. By not giving into discouragement and self-pity!

You can't do this in your own strength; only through Christ who lives within you. Yield to Him and allow Him to live His life through you. *Nancy*

True Success

I was reminded today about how important it is to repeatedly teach my children that success is not measured by how well-educated one becomes, how high a wage one earns, how many friends one has, how much one possesses, how high one's grades are, how attractive or fit one is, or how well one can work.

True success is living a life of godliness, and knowing and pleasing the Lord (Titus 2:12)! *Michelle*

- April 14 -

Like God

"It is I who taught Ephraim to walk, I took them in My arms... and I bent down and fed them" (Hosea 11:3-4 NASB).

What a beautiful picture of our God, who in His mercy bends down to feed and comfort us.

In the same way, mothers reveal the heart of God. When you take your baby in your arms, you are being like God. When you bend down to your little ones to feed and tend to their needs, you are being like God. What a privilege! Delight in it! *Nancy*

Godly Courtship

Where are the folks that believe in courtship today? What is wrong with encouraging our children to stay in the family home until they wed? What is wrong with a young man being serious enough about a young lady to come to the father for permission to get to know her? Isn't this better than dating, or moving out as a young/barely adult? *Michelle*

- April 15 -

Preserved Blameless

What is God's plan for us? He wants to present us unblameable and unreprovable in His sight at the coming of the Lord Jesus (I Corinthians 1:8; Colossians 1:21-22 and I Thessalonians 3:13).

My vision and goal as I raised our children was taken from I Thessalonians 5:23, *"The very God of peace sanctify you wholly; and I pray God your whole spirit and soul and body be **preserved blameless** unto the coming of our Lord Jesus Christ."*

It is not enough to care for our children's physical lives; we have to guard over their soul and spirit. It is a great task that takes our whole life and much prayer. *Nancy*

Obey God Instead of Man

We live in a culture where "whatever floats your boat" is the motto of the day. Yet, if your "boat is floated" by embracing motherhood, children, and your role as a biblical wife, you are often criticized! Basically, whatever "floats your boat" is fine until it involves the uncommon standard of embracing what God embraces. We should feel honored to be condemned for obeying God's Word! *Michelle*

Watch Your Post

Peter encourages the believers to *"Be sober, be vigilant; because your adversary the devil, as a roaring lion, walketh about, seeking whom he may devour: whom resist, steadfast in the faith"* (I Peter 5:8-9).

We cannot let up our guard as we watch over our children. A mother cannot afford to vacate her post. For years the devil has successfully wooed mothers away from their homes in order to sow his tares (Matthew 13:25) and to subtly woo our children away from godliness and into deception. But, when he encounters a praying "watch dog" mother in the home, he has no success. *Nancy*

Culture Shift

I am often amazed at the culture shift we see in attitudes toward family. We constantly hear that things aren't secure enough, couples aren't ready yet, there's not enough financial stability, and many other reasons not to have a baby.

I don't see those excuses in Scripture. I don't read Mary saying she was not ready or Elizabeth saying she was too old. Rather, I see women crying out for babies!

Imagine how the church would grow if the body of Christ all cried out for babies! *Michelle*

- April 17 -

Be a Berean

"But what does the Scripture say?" (Galatians 4:30 NASB). We can all have our own ideas about different subjects, but we must always come back to the premise, *"What does the Scripture say?"*

The doctrine of a subject is what God says about the subject from Genesis to Revelation. Then we get the whole picture. May we be like the Bereans who *"searched the Scriptures daily"* to check if what Paul was saying was correct (Acts 17:11).

May we be lovers of the truth who are not afraid to study what God says rather than assimilating into society's ways. *Nancy*

Babies Give Us a Future!

My baby is growing at breakneck speed and mastering more things every day! With joy and a tinge of sorrow, I watch her move out of babyhood. I love the quote, "Don't baby the old baby; have a new baby instead."

It is so true that babies make love stronger, the home happier, the past forgotten, and the future worth living for. *Michelle*

- April 18 -

Keep on Hoping

*"Now the God of hope fill you with all joy and peace in believing, that ye may **abound in hope**, through the power of the Holy Ghost"* (Romans 15:13). We see a lot of hopelessness; but in the midst of it all, we can hope, for our God is a God of Hope!

Statistics reveal that when a nation no longer hopes, they stop reproducing! Joel Kotkin writes, "The desire to have children is a fundamental affirmation of faith in the future and in values that transcend the individual."

Believers should continue to have children because they have hope. *Nancy*

I'm Amazed!

Twenty years ago today, I made wedding vows and embarked on an adventure for which I was ill-equipped! Now, with a wonderful husband, 11 children, and a lovely married life, I stand amazed. I am so grateful to the One that knows best.

Thank you, Lord for 20 wedded years! They were not all easy, but they were certainly worth it! *Michelle*

- April 19 -

Obliterate, Don't Tolerate!

How do we respond to states legalizing homosexual marriages? Do we accept it and carry on as usual? Should we not do something to protest? Perhaps call our senator or congressman? We cannot stay quiet. Jesus commended the Ephesian church because they could not tolerate evil (Revelation 2:2).

May we be those who hate evil and do not give in to the tolerating spirit of this day. *Nancy*

Look for the Amazing

What are you looking for? Are you looking at the faults, annoyances, and disappointments all around you? Why don't we look for something else—something more helpful and biblical?

Let's actively search for the amazing stories that are happening all around us! God is always doing the most amazing and incredible things, but our eyes have to be wide open to the praiseworthy and the positive in order to see them!

Do not be like the Israelites in the desert. They looked for what they were missing, instead of beholding and praising the miracles they were witnessing right in their very midst! *Michelle*

Labor of Love

I Thessalonians 1:3 talks about our *"labor of love."* Labor is not a vacation, is it? To labor means to work hard and sweat it out. Labor is wearying and uses up our strength.

But, did you know that labor reveals our love? When we labor in our homes to serve our husband and children, it is hard work, but it is also LOVE! Love is not only a nice feeling; it is working hard to serve those we love. Be encouraged today. *Nancy*

Get Your Thinking Straight

"Whatsoever things are TRUE (not assumed), *whatsoever things are HONEST* (not lies), *whatsoever things are JUST* (not unfair), *whatsoever things are PURE* (not defiled), *whatsoever things are LOVELY* (not unenjoyable), *whatsoever things are of GOOD REPORT* (not wicked): *if there be any VIRTUE and if there be any PRAISE* (and of course there is!), *think on these things!"*

And I love how this passage ends, *"And the God of peace shall be with you!"* These are the instructions I need for today from Philippians 4:8-9. Our recipe for peace is to think on these good things. *Michelle*

Apron of Humility

1 Peter 5:5 says, *"Be clothed with humility: for God resisteth the proud, and giveth grace to the humble."* The William's translation says, *"You must all put on the servant's **apron of humility** to one another."*

Isn't that a lovely thought? Humility is like an apron because it denotes the spirit of serving. Put on your humility apron today and enjoy serving your husband and family. *Nancy*

I Want it All

"I only want it all!" This is my new line when I am questioned about my life. I only want to live forever, spending eternity with my Creator in a place that has no sorrow or pain. I only want to be surrounded by lovely children my entire life (via whatever means the Lord supplies—fertility/adoption/fostering/grand-parenting). I only want to be amazingly rich in family, and never impoverished with loneliness.

As a wife, I only want an incredible marriage that is full of life, love, commitment, and passion; and I will continually build into it. I only want to be truly alive, savoring every drop out of each day. I only want to do all that I can do to enhance the lives of those around me, regardless of life's hardships.

I only want people to grasp that they can have it all too! After all, who wouldn't want it all? When you are in love with your life, just as it is, and in love with your faith, you are a powerful witness. Like me, do you only want it all? *Michelle*

- April 22 -

Save Your Family

I sometimes think it is harder to raise children in this wicked 21ˢᵗ century. But nothing has really changed. Evil has always been present.

What about Noah and his family? He didn't have another soul to stand with him. There was not another family in his church fellowship! He had evil influences on every side. And yet, he and his wife raised children who walked in the ways of righteousness in the midst of gross evil. Along with their children, they stood against the tide of the whole world! He saved his family and condemned the world! (Hebrews 11:7). Their confession must have been, *"Let God be true, but every man a liar"* (Romans 3:4).

Can you also stand strong as a family? Can you and your husband raise children who will walk with God in the midst of evil influence? What a great challenge. *Nancy*

Begin with Prayer

What can I do today to bring more love, joy, and peace into the atmosphere of my home? I will start with prayer and my own attitude. I can't control circumstances, but I can attempt to control my own words and actions. Hence, I will definitely begin with prayer. *Michelle*

- April 23 -

Trust His Sufficiency

Are you wondering how you will get through today? Do you feel overwhelmed? The truth is that you will never get through this day on your own. But there is a greater truth—you will get through this day as you acknowledge God is with you. He never leaves you, even when you do not feel His presence. He is your Sufficiency. He is your Tower into which you can run. His everlasting arms are supporting you.

Take hold of this Scripture, *"Not that we are sufficient of ourselves to think anything as of ourselves, but our **sufficiency is of God"** (II Corinthians 3:5). Trust in His sufficiency today. *Nancy*

Why Worry?

Sometimes I stew about issues, trying to come up with my own creative solutions. I waste precious time, pondering over things which I have little control. How silly and counter-productive! I am only a human with limited capacities! Why do I waste my limited resources in worry and fret, especially when I know that my Sovereign Lord is managing all life's affairs?

Luke 12:25-26 NASB says, *"And which of you by worrying can add a single hour to his life's span? If then you cannot do even a very little thing, why do you worry about other matters?"* And Psalm 37:7 says, *"Rest in the Lord, and wait patiently for Him: fret not thyself."* Oh, the peace that comes from implementing God's instructions! Are you wasting time fretting? It's time to hand it over and enjoy life again. *Michelle*

- April 24 -

Don't Allow Lies

Don't overlook any situation when your children lie. John 8:44 NASB says, *"You are of your father the devil... there is no truth in him. Whenever he speaks a lie, he speaks from his own nature, for he is a liar and the father of lies."* When your children lie, they embrace the nature of the devil.

Don't allow them to get into this habit. Deal severely with lying. Make your children understand that *"lying lips are abomination to the Lord"* (Proverbs 12:22). When they lie, they side with the devil and side against God. *Nancy*

Always Climbing

Are you a better wife then you were a year ago? Are you a better mother than you were a year ago? I am sure you are. You are on the grand climb uphill. No slippery slopes for you! Take time to see your growth, rejoice in it, and be patient with yourself. You don't expect your baby to dress herself, do you? Or your pre-schooler to drive to the store? Keep on moving forward! *Michelle*

- April 25 -

What's Your Attitude?

What is our attitude toward children? Even though we love our children, we can often be irritated by them. Jesus said, *"Whoever receives this child in My name receives Me, and whoever receives Me receives Him who sent Me"* (Luke 9:48 NASB).

Isn't it amazing that God says the attitude we have towards children is the attitude we have toward Him? And if we don't want to receive His children, what does He think? *Nancy*

A New Level

Let's take complaining to a whole new level! Picture the following: the Israelites hear the bad report from the spies and voice their concern about going into the Promised Land, crying out in terror and fear. But here is the twist. Let's imagine that instead of deciding to go back to Egypt in a lack of faith, they continue with resolve to trust the Lord, regardless of the circumstances. They walk in FAITH. They agree with Caleb and trust that He who brought them out of Egypt with an outstretched arm would continue to carry them into the Promised Land, even in the face of seemingly insurmountable obstacles! How much toil and pain they would have saved themselves.

Go ahead, voice your complaint if you must, but then, take it to the next level. Confess, "I am afraid, I don't like this, I am struggling, this is awful; BUT (and here is the next level) I put my trust in you, Lord, and I KNOW that you will carry me through." Keep moving forward! *Michelle*

Count Your Blessings

Is there rejoicing in your home today? When God is in the midst there is rejoicing. When God removes His presence, *"joy withers away from the sons of men"* (Joel 1:12). Perhaps you are feeling depressed and don't feel any joy. Please don't rely on your feelings—they come and go and are very deceiving. Begin praising the Lord for who He is, for His salvation, for your husband and children and all His blessings in your life. Joy will soon return.

At your family meal table this evening, ask each one around the table to share a couple of blessings that happened to them today. At prayer time, thank the Lord for these blessings. *Nancy*

The Joy of Brotherhood

Today, my 16-year-old son woke up grumpy, but his three-year-old brother said, "I lay down with you and cuddle." The same three-year-old followed his big brother around relentlessly, asking him to play, sit, eat, and talk with him—often with his hands held together in prayer formation as he pleaded, hour after hour. Both boys are in amazingly cheerful moods and enjoying each other's company immensely. *Michelle*

- April 27 -

Delight to Serve

Jesus said, *"I am among you as He that serveth"* (Luke 22:27). If this was the testimony of Jesus, the Creator of the world, how much more should it be our testimony? It's easy to take on the attitude of "I'm just a slave around this place," isn't it? But, to serve is the spirit of Jesus.

Matthew 10:28 NASB tells us that Jesus *"did not come to be served, but to serve, and to give His life a ransom for many."* Hebrews 3:5 tells us that Moses was a faithful servant in his house. The priests in the tabernacle in the wilderness and the temple in Jerusalem served God in the holy place. Your home is also a holy place to serve God each day.

If we want to be like Jesus, it will be our delight to serve our husband and our children in our home. *Nancy*

I Love to Serve

I find it easy to affirm my love for my husband and children. What I really need to affirm is that I love to serve my family through cooking and cleaning. Do you also need to confess this affirmation? Confess out loud, "I love to serve my family in all household duties." It's good to be reminded that "I love to serve!" *Michelle*

Use Your Strength Wisely

"Give unto the Lord glory and strength" (Psalm 29:1) Where do you give your strength? We are to worship and love God with all our strength.

Also, when God gives us children to nurture and educate for Him, He wants us to give the strength He gives to us each new day to this nation-impacting career. He does not want us to give our strength to lesser things that deplete our energy.

Give your strength to the right cause. *Nancy*

Fight the Battle

Are you struggling today? I am! It is easy to feel frustrated, discontent, grumpy, or critical, yet I know these feelings will only bear the bitterest of fruit!

So the battle is on! I will praise the praiseworthy, I will hold my tongue, I will smile and talk kindly, I will look at my own plank, and I will cast off self-pity, knowing God is Sovereign! This is His will for me, and He knows best! *Michelle*

Refreshing Sleep

One of the side issues of your great career of mothering is tiredness. I remember being so tired when nurturing my little ones (three under 17 months because of twins and four under four at one time) that it was actually painful. But what can we expect when we are doing something so powerful? And we always get through! I am still alive and fit today!

I asked a young mother recently, "What do you do when you feel tired?"

She replied, "I call out to God—and take a nap!"

What a good God we have. He gives His beloved sleep. Go to bed early so you are ready for the new day. When your baby wakes, nurse him in bed and you'll both go off to sleep together. Take a little nap in the afternoon with your baby, and train your other little ones to also have a nap or a "quiet time" on their beds. Don't you love Psalm 3:5? *"I laid me down and slept; I awaked; for **the Lord sustained me**."* *Nancy*

Keep on the Sunny Side!

Great news! We can have control over our attitudes. We can choose how to respond, react, speak and behave! All the other things that we lack control over can be safely left in the hands of our Lord. If we let a poor attitude creep in, we can choose to replace it. The Lord is more than ready to assist us. Stick to the sunny side of the road! I'll see you there! *Michelle*

- April 30 -

Life-Giving Food

God blesses you with sleep to refresh your weariness. He also provides you with life-giving food to replenish your body. Immediately after God ordained the blessing of children, He gave them *"every herb bearing seed, which is upon the face of all the earth"* (Genesis 1:29). God doesn't intend you to live on refined and packaged foods that have no nutritional value to replenish your tired body.

Do you need more energy? Throw out all sugar (which depletes your energy) and all the "whites"—white flour, white bread, white rice, and white pasta. Eat more life-giving and wholesome foods, and watch your energy return. *Nancy*

God's Word Has the Last Say

I read recently, "Teach your children why you believe what you believe. Don't ask them to accept your beliefs blindly. Don't be afraid to teach them to think for themselves. God's Word can withstand the test."

This is encouraging for parents with older children who may be questioning things. Of course, God's word can take it! Why fret? His Spirit can move upon their lives without our worrying. *Michelle*

The Daily Rule

II Chronicles 8:13-14 NASB tells us that *"Solomon offered burnt offerings on the altar of the Lord according to the **daily rule**"* The burnt offerings were to be offered daily, morning and evening. They didn't only do it when they felt like it or only when it fitted in with their plans. They did it daily.

The *"altar of the Lord"* speaks of gathering with our family to pray, worship, and read God's Word together. God intends it to be a "daily rule" in our family life, not haphazard. Ask God to give you His wisdom, and show you how you can order your home in order to make this "daily rule" a blessing in your family. *Nancy*

Unto the Lord

Are you feeling unappreciated? Read Luke 17. Read how only one out of 10 healed men bothered to thank Jesus. And check verse 10. Christ explains, *"When ye shall have done all those things which are commanded you, say, 'We are unprofitable servants: we have done that which was our duty to do.'"*

Remember, regardless of the human lack of affirmation, our service is to the Lord, and HE is our Rewarder. Keep up the great work. *Michelle*

- May 2 -

The Very Least

I have another thought about the *"the daily rule."* I have to confess that life gets busy. I know it is the same for you as you care for your children and keep your home running efficiently. We long to spend time with God, but can't find the time.

I am so grateful for our morning and evening Devotions which we have every day. Two times a day we take time out as a family to pray together and feed from God's Word. Isn't this the very least we can give to God each day? *Nancy*

Warmed to the Core

One of the most moving and powerful parts of my day is when the family gathers at the evening meal, and each member prays out loud to our heavenly Father. It isn't profound or perfect, but it warms me right to my core.

Make sure to implement family prayer in your home, if you haven't already. It is well worth the effort. *Michelle*

- May 3 -

Life-Giving Duty

We read in II Chronicles 8:13-14 that it was also *"the duty"* of the Levites to praise the Lord every morning and evening. Words such as the *"daily rule"* and *"duty"* sound very legalistic, don't they?

Yet, how can it be legalistic to take time out to worship the Lord and have Family Devotions each day when we are reading God's life-giving Word (John 6:63)? How can it be a duty to praise the God of the universe?

Shouldn't it be our greatest privilege? *Nancy*

Are You Pleasing Your Husband?

I often wonder why a wife would want to dress, speak, or behave in any way that bothers her husband. The following quote by J. R. Miller summarizes my sentiment so well.

"She should prize more highly a compliment from her husband's lips than from any other human lips. Therefore, she should reserve for him the sweetest charms."

We all try to please the Lord, but who are we humanly trying to please today? *Michelle*

- May 4 -

Honor is Your Right

God demands honor and respect. He also ordained that parents, who are parenting on His behalf, should receive honor and respect. Disrespect toward parents is also disrespect toward God.

"One of the most dangerous contributions a parent can make toward the spiritual delinquency of his child is a failure to instill within him a wholesome respect for authority. If the parent neglects to set the proper example as an authority figure, or refuses to exercise discipline with love, he might well be rejected as an authority-figure by his child, and thus, by transference, the child ultimately may come to disdain all authority, including the Supreme Authority, God." (From *Surveying the Evidence* by Wayne Jackson, Eric Lyons, and Kyle Butt).

Acknowledge the anointing God has given you as a parent and walk in this anointing and authority. *Nancy*

Jesus' Example

When I think of Christ doing things that were sometimes questionable, such as talking to the Samaritan woman and drinking from her vessel, I am greatly encouraged. It is certainly not culturally correct nowadays to view *all* children (not only my own) as blessings. It is definitely questionable to stay home to raise and teach my family. Thank you, Jesus, for your example! *Michelle*

- May 5 -

A Huge Vision

I am amazed to read about some of the sons of Israel. I Chronicles 12:14-15 NASB says, *"The sons of Gad were captains of the army; he who was least was equal to a hundred and the greatest to a thousand. These are the ones, who crossed the Jordan... when it was overflowing all its banks and they put to flight all those in the valleys, both to the east and to the west."*

What a vision! To raise a son who is equal to a hundred men! Or a son who is equal to a thousand other men! In I Chronicles 26:29-31 we read about *"capable men"* and also *"men of outstanding capability."*

Don't aim for raising sons and daughters that are status quo and like everyone else around. Aim your vision higher. Educate children who will think like God thinks instead of the "dumbing down" spirit of this world. Raise sons who will *"know their God"* and will be *"strong, and do exploits"* (Daniel 11:32). *Nancy*

Keep on Serving

I was feeling tired today, but I was humbled as I read the story of the watchful servants in Luke 12:35-40. It is hard to serve others when weary. Yet, those servants who are watching and alert for the Lord's return will be made to rest, and He will serve them. I can hardly imagine. Me? Served by my God? How incredible and humbling. This thought renews my energy to keep on serving. *Michelle*

Ready Lips

Proverbs 22:17-18 says, *"Bow down thine ear, and hear the words of the wise, and apply thine heart unto my knowledge. For it is a pleasant thing if thou keep them within thee; they shall withal be fitted in thy lips."* We don't hear wise words when we are haughty and proud in spirit. We have to humble our ears to hear. I find myself continually praying, "Lord, please give me ears to hear your words of truth."

I also keep my ears open when I am in the company of wise people. As we listen and wisdom fills our soul, it also fills our lips. Most translations say that wisdom will be *"ready on your lips."* Isn't that lovely? We always have words of wisdom ready to give to our children and those around us.

The Amplified Version says, *"Your lips will be accustomed to confessing them."* Isn't that the picture of the virtuous woman? *"She openeth her mouth with wisdom"* (Proverbs 31:26). *Nancy*

More Siblings, More Fun

Who says children in a large family wish they weren't? My children are so attached to their siblings, they are saddened when one is away from home. They all compete for attention from the baby, and they can't wait to tell each other their stories and events. To them, the larger the audience, the better. Plus, there is always someone to play with. *Michelle*

- May 7 -

Backbone of the Nation

Mother, you are the backbone of the nation! You are the greatest threat to those who want to turn this nation away from God's ways. You may often feel snowed under, but I want to remind you that as you pour out your life to nurture, train, and educate your children, you determine the course of this nation and even the world.

There is no career that is more important than what you are doing as a mother. May you be daily strengthened and anointed by God's almighty power. *Nancy*

Your Husband's Crown

Proverbs 12:4 states, *"A virtuous woman is a crown to her husband."* Are you adorning your husband today with your noble, cheerful, and loving character? He loves to see you smile. You can make his day! What a privilege to breathe life into your husband. *Michelle*

- May 8 -

You Are a Nourisher

God has anointed you to be a nourisher! You nourish your babies with nutrient-filled, life-giving milk from your breasts, and they grow into beautiful bonny babies.

You continue to nourish your children with wisdom and life-giving words that pour from your mouth. You are a Word-nourisher, daily filling your children with God's life-giving truth, which has the power to keep them from falling (I Timothy 4:6 and Hebrews 4:12).

Think "nourishment" and you'll be right in the perfect will of God. *Nancy*

More Communication

Who says having a large family means less time for communication and "connecting" with each other? A truth I have learned from having a large family is that there is always someone around to notice you.

More people in the family necessitates more communication, which leads to greater interconnectedness among all members. *Michelle*

- May 9 -

Strange, Isn't It?

Hosea 8:12 NASB says, *"Though I wrote for him ten thousand precepts of My law, they are regarded as a strange thing."* What is normal in the Bible is now strange to people who confess they are believers.

God says children are a blessing, and yet, many Christians do not want more than one or two "blessings!" They think it is strange! They frown at homeschoolers, and yet allow their children to be indoctrinated with humanism!

Isn't that strange? *Nancy*

Walk in Truth

Are you beating yourself up over something? The truth is that victory is yours. Your Mighty Deliverer is forever tending to you in love and compassion beyond comprehension!

It's time to walk in truth and not get stuck in the rut of despair! You are doing an amazing job even though it's not all perfect! Enjoy your day as though it were perfect! *Michelle*

Guard Your Own Vineyard

J. R. Miller writes, "A mother had better be missed in the church and at the public meetings—than be missed in her own household."

I am reminded of the words of the Shulamite in Song of Solomon 1:6, *"They made me the keeper of the vineyards; but my own vineyard have I not kept."* Don't let society, or even pressure from the church, keep you from keeping your own vineyard.

You will often be pressured. Do you notice the words, *"they **made** me"*? Stand true to your calling. Watch over your own vineyard, not someone else's vineyard. *Nancy*

My Catch!

I used to have the attitude that I was the "real catch" in my marriage. The interesting thing is that my marriage was terrible during that time.

When I realized that my husband was, in fact, a "real catch," my marriage became amazing! Attitude and perspective sure make a humungous impact. Do not underestimate them, and do not be deceived. *Michelle*

- May 11 -

The Puzzle Fits

Ephesians 5:17 says, *"Be ye not unwise, but **understanding** what the will of the Lord is."* God's ultimate will for us is to be sanctified, "set apart" for His service, and to be conformed to the image of His Son. His functional will for us as mothers is to embrace the career of mothering and nurturing, for this is the way God has created us, innately and physically.

The word, "understanding" in the Greek literally means "to collect the pieces of the puzzle and put them together." When we embrace God's will for us as mothers, we find the puzzle fits. We no longer live in frustration and confusion as to who we are meant to be. *Nancy*

Gracious Words

In reference to Jesus, Luke 4:22 ESV says, *"All spoke well of Him and marveled at the **gracious** words that were coming from His mouth."*

May gracious words come from our lips today. The Hebrew word is *charis* and means "to favor, to show kindness, compassion, mercy, and long-suffering." May we be known for our gracious speech. *Michelle*

Incalculable!

May I remind you, dear mother, that you are a Life-giver, a Nurturer, a Nourisher, a Director of Home Affairs, a Home Builder, a Nation Builder, an Educator, an Encourager, an Arrow Polisher, a Memory Maker, an Influencer of Future Generations, and a Molder of Children for Heaven?

Your worth is incalculable! There is no career that has the backing of God more than motherhood!

Be filled with joy as you mother your children today. Walk in the power of your anointing. Keep up the good work. *Nancy*

Extra Doses of Love

Today, I am privileged to celebrate my daughter's 18th birthday! I love celebrations and special days, don't you?

Although we should cherish each other every day, a special day gives us reason to go over the top with extra doses of love and praise! We get to break out of the ordinary and pour out blessings on our girl! What fun! *Michelle*

- May 13 -

One Brave Man

Do know the story of Ebed-melech, the Ethiopian? When he heard that the palace officials had put Jeremiah the prophet in the dungeon and that he was sinking in the thick mire (and would most probably die), he rushed to the king and boldly pleaded for permission to rescue Jeremiah. Ebed-melech took his life into his hands to stand up for right. He could have landed in the dungeon himself, because the king had just given the palace officials permission to do what they liked with Jeremiah! But Ebed-melech was not a wimp! He was not afraid of the consequences. He acted righteously and saved Jeremiah. It only took one brave man!

Many times people are accused wrongly. Are we afraid to stand up for them in case we face the same consequences? Many times we face an evil situation. Will we stand against the evil? May God save us from being those who turn a blind eye because we would rather not be involved. May we always stand against injustice and wrongdoing. Let's teach our children to support and stand by those who are accused falsely. Read the story to your children in Jeremiah 38:6-13 and 39:16-18 and teach them to be brave soldiers for righteousness. *Nancy*

Shaping the World

As you raise up the next generation, you are doing the mightiest of works! You are the most privileged of women! You are shaping, and impacting the world with your mothering! Embrace your high position with renewed zest today! *Michelle*

- May 14 -

Beautiful Things

Do you love beautiful things? I do. In Titus 2: 3-5, older women are commanded to teach the younger women "good" things. The word "good" is *kalos* and means "beautiful and valuable."

When you are obedient and loving to your husband, it is a "beautiful" thing. When you love your children, you are doing a "good" thing. When you embrace the role God has given you to run your home efficiently, and train, teach, and nurture your children, you are doing something that is very "valuable." It is valuable to God, to your husband, to your children, and to future generations.

Dear mother, you are worth more than rubies and precious gems! You are invaluable! *Nancy*

Say No to Status Quo!

Who wants status quo? Is that really living the abundant life? Christ didn't live His life on earth trying to be like everyone else. He did what He knew He had to do, even when condemned and ridiculed.

Isn't that truly living? Doing what you know to do even if you are the only one doing it? Isn't that being the salt and the light? Isn't that the abundant life?

Go ahead, shake up the status quo! *Michelle*

- May 15 -

Feeding Lips

Proverbs 10:21 says, *"The lips of the righteous feed many."* I long for this to be my testimony, but in order to have feeding lips, I must first feed my soul. I want God's Word to be not only in my heart, but in my mouth, ready to feed whomever is around. All mothers need feeding lips. Not only do we feed hungry bodies, but our children have hungry souls and spirits, too.

What a tragic thing to be faithful in feeding our children's bodies so they are robust and strong and yet they grow up with tiny starved souls and spirits because we have failed to feed their inward man. Our children's "inner man" needs feeding more than their "outer man." I like to tell my children the statement I read of a great Chinese Christian who confessed, "No Bible; no breakfast!" He would never feed his physical body until he first fed his spirit.

Be a "lip feeder" today, richly feeding your children and those around you with wisdom and truth. *Nancy*

Antidote to Self-Pity

Mark 10:45 NASB says, *"For even the Son of Man did not come to be served, but to serve."* Serving others is a perfect way to emulate Christ. It is also a perfect antidote to self-pity! I find it hard to feel sorry for myself when I put my heart into serving and blessing someone else! There is always a blessing for us when we do things God's way! *Michelle*

- May 16 -

A Great Heritage

I received an email from my dear friend, Sally Ott, mother of 16 children and currently 83 grandchildren and great-grandchildren.

She writes, "Was it all worth it? Yes! At age 77, I can tell you that it was all worth it—every cry, every diaper, every sleep lost, every evening-out missed, and every tear! I would do it all over again. What did I miss? Nothing! What did I gain? Very interesting people who love me and a peaceful home always filled with laughter."

What a heritage! *Nancy*

Adjust Your Expectations

Paul confessed, *"I have learned, in whatsoever state I am, therewith to be content"* (Philippians 4:11b).

We set ourselves up for failure when we expect things to go a certain way. It can be easy to be grumpy, or discontent when our expectations are not met.

We must adjust our expectations to *"whatever situation,"* and adjust our response to *"be content."* It's a good thing we have God's supernatural power to help us! *Michelle*

Rejoicing Homes

*"You shall rejoice in **all** the good which the Lord your God has given you and your household"* (Deuteronomy 26:11 NASB). Count the blessings God has given you in your home today. Rejoice in them. Rejoice in the children God has given you. It is so easy to complain and whine, but God wants you to rejoice.

Can you imagine the impact of REJOICING HOMES all over the nation? Could your home be known as a "rejoicing home"? This evening at Family Devotions we sang together the old hymn, "Count your blessings, name them one by one, and it will surprise you what the Lord hath done!" I think we need to sing it more frequently. *Nancy*

Start Where You Are!

Wherever you are at today, start there! Does your marriage need a boost? Plan a romantic evening. Do some habits need changing? Pick one and begin to conquer it. Is your house needing some work? Start with one closet, or one room. Is a child out of control? Pick a discipline issue, and begin an overhaul.

May the Lord multiply your efforts as you trust in Him for victory. *Michelle*

- May 18 -

Learn from Jesus

Jesus said, *"I am gentle and humble in heart, and you will find rest for your souls"* (Matthew 11:29). How we need to learn from Jesus. As we allow His gentle and humble spirit to fill our lives, not only will we find rest in our souls, but we bring rest to our whole family.

When we hold on to pride and stubbornness, we produce a tense and turbulent atmosphere. When we seek to be gentle, rest pervades the home. *Nancy*

Heart Warmers

I am looking out the window and watching my teenage boy digging up a bush that I want moved. He is assisted by training two younger brothers on how to get the job done. Three other children are taking turns pulling the youngest family member in the wagon. It warms my heart.

Although siblings do not always get along, what would they do without each other? *Michelle*

God Is with You NOW!

God revealed Himself to Moses as I AM THAT I AM! (Exodus 3:14). That says it. No one can question God's purposes, for He is I AM THAT I AM. No one can question His counsel, for He is Jehovah, and His thoughts are far above our thoughts.

But more than that, He is I AM today. He is I AM in the situation you face right at this moment. He is not only the faithful God of the past and the eternal future, but the God of the moment. Now! He is I AM with you in your kitchen right now, with all your frustrations and the needs of your little children and teens.

God said to Moses, *"Say unto the children of Israel, I AM hath sent me unto you."* I AM comes to you right now. Acknowledge His presence with you at this "special" moment. Every situation, no matter how frustrating or difficult, is sacred when I AM is with you. *Nancy*

Living My Cinderella Dream

In an attempt to entice us girls to continue our studies in math and science, our high-school teachers told us, "Don't believe in the Cinderella Dream! Many girls think they will get swept off their feet, marry and live happily ever after."

I obtained a post-secondary degree, and yet, here I am most definitely living the Cinderella dream with my handsome prince! And, I wouldn't want to be doing anything else! *Michelle*

Every Day of the Week

Isaiah 41:10 certainly is a wonderful promise. Did you realize there are seven promises in this Scripture, one for every day of the week? You can take one each day, and thank God for His constant presence with you, no matter what you are going through.

Fear not on Sunday,
I am with you on Monday,
Be not dismayed on Tuesday,
I am thy God on Wednesday,
I will strengthen you on Thursday,
I will help you on Friday,
I will uphold you with the right hand of my righteousness on Saturday.

Praise God for His daily faithfulness and for His mercies, which are new every morning. *Nancy*

Is Your Husband Neglected?

Is your husband feeling a tad neglected? It can be so easy to get caught up in mothering above every other role! After all, we are our children's advocates. They are dependent upon us, often unable to do much on their own, especially when they are young. Yet, don't forget to take some time today to also be a loving wife, as well as an excellent mother. I know I need to. *Michelle*

- May 21 -

Make It Happen

Ladies who come to *Above Rubies* retreats know that I believe in the power of affirming the truths of God's Word and confessing powerful affirmations.

One of my favorite affirmations is, "Things don't just happen: you have to make them happen!" I relate this to every area of my life. Creating a peaceful and happy atmosphere doesn't just happen. You have to make it happen! Don't let your home evolve into chaos, which can easily happen if you let it!

You determine the atmosphere and order of your home. Take the first step today to make something happen. *Nancy*

Respond to Your Beloved

"I have taken off my robe—must I put it on again? I have washed my feet—must I soil them again?" (Song of Solomon 5:3 NIV).

The Shulamite asks herself these questions, and in so doing, misses an opportunity. She, in fact, ends up in trouble (see verse 7).

Can we respond without first asking about the inconvenience it may cause? We may find ourselves being richly blessed. *Michelle*

- May 22 -

Exceedingly Joyful

Paul confessed, *"I am **exceeding** joyful in all our tribulation"* (II Corinthians 7:4). What is our confession? Most of us complain when we go through tribulation. We hardly face tribulation in this country, but it may be advisable to get in practice for when it may not be so easy.

Let's seek to be joyful even when we face small hardships. Not only joyful, but **exceedingly** joyful! What a difference this would make in our attitude and the example we give to our children. *Nancy*

Show Respect

Showing respect can be difficult, especially when someone's actions do not seem worthy. When I am in this spot, I remind myself that my good behavior did not bring about my salvation. If that were the case, I would fail.

I am saved by the grace of God. Surely then, I can show respect, regardless of the worthiness of the actions. After all, it is the person I am respecting, not the behavior. *Michelle*

- May 23 -

Embrace Motherhood

Every mother loves her children, but not every mother loves motherhood. Although they adore their children, many mothers seek to run from the career of motherhood. They have been indoctrinated to think there are more important careers. However, the secret to entering into the joy and glory of motherhood is to acknowledge that it is THE DIVINE CALLING God has given to you. Motherhood is not something to run from as the liberalists advocate, but to EMBRACE!

Start off every day confessing aloud, I LOVE MOTHERHOOD. Tell your children that you LOVE being their mother. You will be amazed how this practice will change your attitude, your mothering, and your whole household! *Nancy*

Leave a Legacy

It is my birthday today. Birthdays are a great time to reflect on the legacy we leave. We touch many lives each day, always leaving memories and impressions. The older I get, the more aware I am of how fleeting time is! Every moment must be savored and used wisely. More and more, I hope to build memories that give a firm foundation and a secure footing.

I want to leave an intentional legacy, not just any legacy! I want my life to make people hunger and yearn for the Christian way of life. I want them to see Christ in me as the source of my faith, enabling me to offer love, mercy, grace, and wisdom. Thankfully, these are all at my disposal from the Father's heavenly hand. With His help, my legacy, and yours, will be blessed and fruitful. *Michelle*

- May 24 -

Take Your Children on a Journey

One of the most profound things we can do for ourselves, and the lives of our children, is to search out the attributes of God. We have a responsibility to find Him, although our finite minds will never comprehend His infinity. He is all-sufficient, all-powerful, all-wise, and all-knowing. His attributes would take pages to list.

C. H. Spurgeon writes, "There is something exceedingly improving to the mind in a contemplation of the Divinity. It is a subject so vast, that all our thoughts are lost in its immensity; so deep, that our pride is drowned in its infinity."

Take your children on a journey of finding God. Get out your concordance, taking one attribute at a time, and read the Scriptures about it to your children. Discuss them together. This is the greatest study you will ever embark upon as a family. *Nancy*

More Babies

Is there anything more beautiful than a baby? Is there anything that brings a smile to the face quicker than a baby? Is there anything nicer to touch than a baby? I think not.

I hope my life is filled with babies—my babies, my sibling's babies, my children's babies, by grandchildren's babies, and babies in my community. Life is too short to let too much time pass without experiencing a baby. I vote for more! *Michelle*

- May 25 -

A True Understanding

We continue to meditate on knowing God. We adore His love and mercy, His longsuffering and patience, His justice and truth, but have you noticed that we rarely think about His wrath? It is not even church culture to think of such a thing.

And yet, did you know that there are more Scripture references to God's wrath and fury than there are to His mercy? Without this attribute, He could not be good (Romans 2:4-5).

Speaking as the Judge, God states in Psalm 50:21 NAB, *"You thought that I was just like you."* I have always been challenged by this Scripture. How dare I bring God down to my estimation of Him!

I do not want to worship a God of my own imagination, but who He truly is. How careful we must be in teaching our children a full and true understanding of God and not our finite mindset of what we would like Him to be. *Nancy*

Provisions Arrive!

Who says having a large family is unaffordable? I have watched, in utter amazement, how the Lord has provided in the most unexpected and unanticipated ways for our family. As our family grew, the provisions arrived. The provisions didn't come first—the babies did. Deuteronomy 28:4 tells us that the fruit of the womb is blessed first, and then the crops. *Michelle*

You Are the Best Teacher

Do you think you are incapable of teaching your children? Dear mother, you are the best teacher in the world. God ordained you to teach, and He gave you this ability. You begin teaching your children from the moment they are born. In their first few years, you teach them everything about life—how to talk, walk, etiquette, to understand God's world, and all the basic foundations of life. And you are still the best teacher for the rest of their lives.

God reminds children, *"Do not forsake your mother's teaching"* (Proverbs 1:8). Whose teaching? The Sunday school teacher's? The state school teacher's? No, it is the mother's teaching. Again, in Proverbs 6:20-22 NASB we read, *"Do not forsake the teaching your mother; bind them continually on your heart; tie them around your neck. When you walk bout, they will guide you; when you sleep, they will watch over you; and when you awake, they will talk to you."* That's the most powerful and influential teaching I have read about.

You can do it, mother. You are the best! You have been ordained for the task! *Nancy*

More Children, More Blessings

Who says having a large family puts too much strain on a marriage? We found that the more children we had, the more unity and strength we had to have as a couple. More children meant more reasons to be communicating and supporting each other. In our experience, the children solidified us and forced us both to be less selfish. *Michelle*

- May 27 -

Undeserving Goodness

Today is my birthday. What a blessing to look back over many years and see the guiding hand of God upon my life and the life of our family. I didn't always see it, especially when facing difficult times, but looking back, I see the goodness of God. You will too, for no matter what happens in your life, God is working it out for good.

I love Joshua's words in Joshua 23:14, *"Not one thing hath failed of all the good things which the Lord your God spake concerning you; all are come to pass unto you, and not one thing hath failed thereof."* Also Moses' confession in I Kings 8:56, *"There hath not failed one word of all His good promise."* The word "failed" is *naphal* and actually means "fallen." God will not let one of His promises to you fall! *Nancy*

Keep Practicing

I find that one of the most beautiful things about the fruit of the Spirit is that the more you practice them, the easier they become. I especially love self-control and patience. Every time I manage to show some, the easier it is the next time I need them.

The Lord is faithful to help us in times of need. He honors our efforts and multiplies our fruit. How wonderful. *Michelle*

- May 28 -

Spit Them Out!

"For the ear tests words, as the palate tastes food" (Job 34:3 NASB).
Our taste determines what we eat. We spit out nasty foods!

In the same way, we do not have to accept every thought that comes
into our head. Learn to sift the words you hear.

The devil tries to pull us down and immobilize us by putting negative
thoughts in our mind—deceiving, doubting, discouraging, and
despairing thoughts! Don't accept them. Spit them out! *Nancy*

Declutter Your Mind

I am always amazed at how often our home needs de-cluttering! How
is it that "stuff" constantly accumulates and takes over?

I am afraid it is the same with our minds. Our thoughts can become
cluttered with lies and deceptions, and we can so easily succumb to the
prevalent notions that surround us.

"Oh Lord, help us today to de-clutter our minds and see where we may
be straying from your truth. Amen." *Michelle*

- May 29 -

Shame or Delight?

Proverbs 29:15 says, *"The rod and reproof give wisdom: but a child left to himself bringeth his mother to shame."* The NASB translates it, *"A child who gets his own way brings shame to his mother."* Do you want children who bring you shame or give you delight?

It's easy to let our children have their own way, especially when they harp on and on. We give in to them when they want something when we are out shopping. We give in to stop their whining. But what are we doing? Training them for selfishness and getting ourselves ready to face shame.

We must train our children in God's way. It is lazy mothering to let our children have their own way. Will you be a diligent or lazy mother today? *Nancy*

Put On Your Armor

Are you wearing your full armor today? We desperately need the belt of truth, the breastplate of righteousness, the shield of faith, the helmet of salvation, and the sword of the Spirit, which is the word of God, in order to stand firm in this world. When we couple this with prayer, we are well fitted for our tasks.

> *"Take time today to read and pray,*
> *See how much smoother is your day."*

Michelle

- May 30 -

Strengthened for Patience

How many times during the day do we have to rule our spirit? It is easy to let go, give into our emotions, and fly off the handle! But, what are we teaching our children? We show them a picture of an undisciplined spirit.

Colossians 1:11 says, *"Strengthened with all might, according to His glorious power."*

Why does God strengthen us with His might and power? To do great and mighty exploits? No. Let's read the rest of the Scripture, *"Unto all patience and longsuffering with joyfulness; giving thanks unto the Father."*

The Holy Spirit dwells in you mightily to strengthen you to be patient and longsuffering. Isn't that amazing? *Nancy*

Watch Out for Robbers

Are you being robbed? Perhaps your joy is missing? Our culture tries to rob us of our God-given role and the joy that comes with fulfilling it. Be robbed no longer!

Live counter-culture and be proud of it. Who cares what the world says? Nothing pays better than the love and affection of a child and the peace of living in God's will. *Michelle*

Drudgery or Delight?

Proverbs 31:13 tells us that the "above rubies" woman *"worketh willingly with her hands."* The NASB translation says she performs it *"with delight."*

No matter how menial the task, she tackles it with delight.

We can choose to work grudgingly or willingly. We can look upon everything we do as drudgery or delight. Which will you choose today? *Nancy*

Let Him Know Today

I haven't had much quality time with my husband lately. *"I am my Beloved's, and my Beloved is mine"* (Song of Solomon 6:3) keeps going through my mind. I must need the reminder! To have a beloved at all is a gift, and to be beloved is a privilege!

It's time to prioritize and let our spouses know how loved they are! Marriages need tending. *Michelle*

- June 1 -

Slaves of Human Opinion?

C. H. Spurgeon wrote, "Are we not in Christ made kings to reign upon the earth? How then, can we be the servants of custom, the slaves of human opinion?"

Are you a slave, or are you free? Do you live by God's principles or the custom of this world? Are you allowing God to transform your mind with His thoughts or are you letting the *"world around you squeeze you into its own mould"* (Romans 12:1-2, J. B. Phillips)?

When people say derogatory remarks to you about having more than the usual two children, don't be intimidated. You are not living by humanistic standards, but by the eternal truths of God's Word. Never be ashamed of God's plan. It's better than man's. *Nancy*

Keep Your Home in Order

In a busy family, it is easy for things to become unorganized and chaotic. God's orderliness shows us the better way. My home recently needed a good re-organizing in order to bring peace and a better quality of life. School and daily life go so much better when everything is where it should be. It is time well invested. *Michelle*

- June 2 -

Lean on the Rock

Do you sometimes feel weak and incapable of the great career of raising your children for God? It's true that when we lean on our own resources and the "wisdom of Egypt," they often cave in (II Kings 18:21 and Isaiah 36:6). In fact, it will pierce us!

However, we have a Rock on which to lean who is unchangeable, immovable, and totally trustworthy. We can put our whole weight upon Him (even with all our burdens piled high), and it will not move Him. He will take the strain for us.

We can cry out with David, *"When my heart is overwhelmed: lead me to the rock that is higher than I. For Thou hast been a **shelter** for me, and a **strong tower** from the enemy"* (Psalm 61:2-3). *Nancy*

Death and Life in the Tongue

I am always amazed at the power of words. The Lord chooses to speak to us primarily through His written word, and He reminds us in Matthew 12:37, *"For by thy words thou shalt be justified, and by thy words thou shalt be condemned."*

Proverbs 18:21 also reminds us that *"Death and life are in the power of the tongue."* Let's use our words to bless, build up, and give life. *Michelle*

- June 3 -

More Power than Congress

At Family Devotions last night my husband asked the question, "Who has more power to move the mighty hand of God—Congress and parliaments or families praying together?"

We know the answer to this question, don't we? And yet we still don't pray! How the adversary tries to keep us from wielding this great power. As we daily pray together we can impact nations! God is looking for families to call upon His name together (Jeremiah 10:25).

Will you be one of these families? *Nancy*

Be a Life-Giver

Women bring forth life and not only through childbirth. We bring life into the home all the time. Our positive presence, our exuberance, our attitude, our servant ministry, our life-giving words, our smiles, our prayers, our energy, our lovely appeal, and our compassion, our grace, and our mercy all give forth LIFE!

How will you bring life into your realm today? *Michelle*

- June 4 -

Change Our Thinking

This morning at *Family Devotions* we were challenged by the words of II Corinthians 12:10, *"Therefore I take **pleasure** in infirmities, in reproaches, in necessities, in persecutions, in distresses for Christ's sake: for when I am weak, then am I strong."*

We need to change our thinking, don't we? How easy it is to complain about little things we face in the home, and yet we are not even suffering persecution!

What is your attitude to your weaknesses, hardships, and calamities you face? What is mine? I am challenged. *Nancy*

Watch Them Bloom

The words we speak make such a huge impact. Let's use them to build up everyone in our home. Encouragement and praise are the soil in which we thrive. The more positive things we hear, the more positive we become.

Let's encourage and praise our husband and children, and watch them bloom beautifully. I've tried it and it works. *Michelle*

- June 5 -

Goodbye Doubts

When questions or doubts come into your mind, you don't have to guess their origin. They come straight from the Father of lies whose intention is to deceive you. When your thoughts are filled with "If, Can, Has, But, and How?" you'll know who is putting these thoughts in your mind.

The first temptation from the devil was, *"Has God said?"* Adam and Eve's sin started with listening to a doubt. The Israelites continually questioned God, *"Can God furnish a table in the wilderness? ...Can He give bread also? Can He provide flesh for His people?"* (Psalm 78:18-20). God's anger rose up against them because of their doubts and unbelief in His omnipotency. The devil tried his same tactics on Jesus Himself. *"If Thou be the Son of God..."* (Matthew 4:3-11).

Put out of your mind all "ifs" and "buts." They are the devil's vernacular. Instead, confess with Job, *"Though He slay me, yet will I trust Him"* (Job 13:15). *Nancy*

Increase, Not Decrease

Why do some Christians think it is better not to bring a child into this sinful world? How can good overcome evil if God's people do not raise godly seed? God never told His people to decrease, only to increase! *Michelle*

- June 6 -

Help Me to Be Kind

One of God's attributes is kindness. The Hebrew word is *chesed*, which is one of the most powerful words in the Old Testament. The meaning is much bigger than our English word of kindness. It means unfailing love, benevolence, goodness, grace (which we don't deserve), mercy, loyalty, and strength.

The amazing thing is that God wants us to reveal His same *chesed* kindness to one another. It gets even more personal when we read the description of the virtuous woman in Proverbs 31:26, *"She openeth her mouth with wisdom; and in her tongue is the law of **kindness**."* Yes, the word is *chesed*.

Can you imagine what our homes would be like if we daily and constantly demonstrated and spoke words of kindness to our husband and children? *Nancy*

Always Do Him Good

I am thinking today about Proverbs 31:11-12, *"The heart of her husband doth safely trust in her, so that he shall have no need of spoil. She will do him good and not evil all the days of her life."*

I need to consistently work on being kind. This would do so much to allow my husband's heart to safely trust me to always do him good. This is both a beautiful and attainable goal, because *"I can do all things through Christ which strengthens me"* (Philippians 4:13). *Michelle*

- June 7 -

A Cheerful Countenance

Proverbs 15:13 says, *"A merry heart maketh a cheerful countenance."*
What an amazing difference it makes to the home when the mother has
a cheerful countenance! How can you do it when you feel grumpy,
tired, and irritable?

Dear mother, did you know that you can change your countenance by
the attitude of your heart? It's your attitude, not your feelings. What a
sad household when you live by your feelings. You are miserable,
your children are miserable, and your husband doesn't want to be
around!

Come on now, lift up your head. God is on the throne. He is your
strength and your joy. **Against everything you feel**, acknowledge His
joy that dwells in you because He lives in you. Praise the Lord. Count
your blessings. And your countenance will change. *Nancy*

The Ripple Effect

How's the atmosphere in your home today? Is it filled with joy, peace,
love, contentment, and acceptance? Or is there anger, frustration,
strife, and resentment?

Well, you know what to do to, don't you? As Nancy loves to say,
"Things don't just happen—you have to make them happen!"

Start with yourself, and the "ripple effect" will affect the whole house.
A fire starts with a spark, and you are that spark. *Michelle*

- June 8 -

Sunny Faces

I like the MLB translation of Proverbs 15:13 which says, *"A happy heart makes the face look sunny."* What does a sunny face look like? It's a smiling face!

"But, I don't feel like smiling," you complain. Once again, it's nothing to do with how you feel. You must get out of this habit of living by your feelings. It is a depleting way to live.

One pioneer woman said, "Self-pity is the lowest state to which a woman's mind can fall."

So forget those morbid feelings. Put on a smile. You can do it! Start smiling, and you'll be amazed at how different you feel. And you'll be amazed at what happens in your home. Not only will your face be sunny, but your home will be filled with sunny faces. *Nancy*

Brighten Your Day

A sunny disposition can brighten up the bleakest of days! The most attractive, enjoyable, and beautiful people are those that have warm and positive attitudes. May you be one of those people today. God bless you mightily in your endeavors. *Michelle*

- June 9 -

Unending Feast

I haven't finished yet! Moffat's translation of Proverbs 15:13 says, *"A cheerful heart is an unending feast."* A feast is where you feed sumptuously. No scantiness at a feast. A feast is where you enjoy people, laugh, and smile. No morbidity at a feast. God wants your life in your home to be a continual feast of joy.

It all begins with the state of your heart. Not the "feelings" of your heart, but how you determine the state of your heart. Don't allow your feelings to rule you; instead you rule the state of your heart.

Thank God for His blessings. Thank God that Christ, who is Joy and Peace, reigns in your heart. Acknowledge the life of Christ within you and radiate joy and thankfulness whether you feel like it or not. Instead of living a scanty life, enjoy an unending feast that sustains and satiates your soul. *Nancy*

Happy Smiles

Why wait for circumstances to be exactly how we'd like them to be? We can be truly happy and celebrate life no matter what! Life, even simply breathing, is an absolute gift. Each day is a new adventure! Embrace your life today, and enjoy it with a thankful heart and a happy smile. *Michelle*

- June 10 -

Source of Peace

My daughter, Evangeline, popped in a little while ago. "I have a new revelation," she said. "Motherhood is equated with joy (Psalm 113:9). Children are joy-bringers! They fill our lives with joy. But do they give us peace? Well, children are loud! Children exert energy! It is God who gives peace!"

God says in Isaiah 66:12, *"I will extend peace to her like a river."* God extends peace to you. Find joy in your children, but look to God for your peace. *Nancy*

God Never Complains

I caught myself getting tired of the "drudgery," of doing the same old chores again and again.

The Lord reminded me that He, too, does the same things for me over and over again. He forgives my same sins over and over. He hears my pleas and answers me over and over again. He comforts me over and over again. He is patient with me over and over again.

Suddenly, "drudgery" has a whole new meaning! I'm a smiling girl now! *Michelle*

- June 11 -

The "D" Ammunition

How can we effectively resist the enemy? God gives us the strategy in Numbers 33:52-53 NASB.

> *"**Drive out** all the inhabitants of the land,*
> ***Destroy all** of their engraved stones,*
> ***Destroy all** their molded images,*
> ***Demolish all** their high places,*
> ***Dispossess** the inhabitants of the land..."*

Don't compromise with the enemy in your home. Drive him out in the power of the name of Jesus, and establish righteousness in your home. *Nancy*

Building Blocks

When we build our families with family meals and devotions, we strengthen our marriage. We also give godly examples to generations to follow. What on earth could be more powerful, significant, or rewarding? *Michelle*

- June 12 -

The Beauty of Jesus

Moses prayed in Psalm 90:17, *"Let the beauty of the Lord our God be upon us."* We would all like to be beautiful, wouldn't we? Beauty is delightful to behold. In fact, "delight" is the meaning of this word in this Scripture.

More than anything else, God wants His beauty to be upon us. He wants our children to learn of His beauty and character as they watch our lives. He wants the world to see His beauty through us, for this is the way He has planned for them to get a glimpse of Him.

His beauty is His presence in our lives. I love to pray these lines...

> *"Let the beauty of Jesus be seen in me,*
> *All His wondrous compassion and purity.*
> *O Thou Spirit Divine, all my nature refine,*
> *'Till the beauty of Jesus be seen in me."*

Nancy

Worthwhile Ideals

Some things are definitely worth our time. Building up our marriage. Enjoying our children. Loving our family and friends. Serving others. Eating real food. May you continue to do an amazing job as you pursue these worthwhile passions. The world is watching and learning.
Michelle

Perfect Peace

Would you like to know my favorite Scripture? It is Isaiah 26:3-4, *"Thou wilt keep him in perfect peace, whose mind is stayed on Thee: because he trusteth in Thee. Trust ye in the Lord forever: for in the Lord JEHOVAH is everlasting strength."* Because it is a favorite, I have memorized it, so it is always with me.

What is perfect peace? The true Hebrew rendering is "peace, peace," meaning a double portion of peace. It is God's peace, which is undisturbable. Don't you love that? Nothing, no matter how traumatic, disturbs God! Because He is your God and dwells in you, you can also live in undisturbable peace.

But there are two things you have to do: 1) Focus your thoughts upon the Lord. If all your thoughts are upon your problem and the trauma you are facing, you will not experience peace. 2) Trust totally in the Lord. If your trust is in man or you are trying to solve your problem with your own limited capacity, you will continue to live in stress. Try God's way. *Nancy*

Nation's Powerhouse

Remember, if you weren't doing anything worthwhile, there'd be nothing to attack! You are engaged in a mighty work and few things can compare with it. The family unit is the powerhouse of the nation, and the task is crucial. *Michelle*

- June 14 -

Which one?

An *Above Rubies* reader emailed this little poem to me. It hangs in the home of her mother-in-law, who has 53 grandchildren!

> *I have two natures in my breast,*
> *One is foul, the other blest.*
> *One I love and one I hate,*
> *The one I feed will dominate!*
> *The one that most my children see,*
> *I'll soon find out; they're just like me!*

Which one are you feeding today? *Nancy*

As Good as Your Attitude

The atmosphere of your home is only as good as your attitude! Believe the truth and toss out any lies that try to bring you down! You are doing the mightiest work, and God mightily equips you for the task. Believe it, and it becomes a self-fulfilling prophecy. *Michelle*

- June 15 -

You Have a Resting Place

Do you have turmoil in your life? Are you bowed down with worry? God's Word comes to you today: *"Return unto thy rest, O my soul"* (Psalm 116:7).

Christ Jesus is your rest. Look to Him. Trust in Him. Thank Him for His rest that fills your soul. When you dwell on your problem, you will stay in a state of anxiety; when you trust in Christ, you will experience true rest.

God told His people that they "have forgotten their resting place" (Jeremiah 50:6). Don't forget you have a resting place. *Nancy*

Discipline for Peace

Is the atmosphere of your home not as peaceful as you would like? In our house, things unravel quickly when our lives whirl out of schedule. We need to execute consistent training and discipline in order for peace to return. A peaceful home is a well-disciplined home! I am sure this is the key reason why the Scriptures exhort us to discipline and train our children—so that peace can reign! *Michelle*

- June 16 -

Daily Faithfulness—Big Reward!

What does it mean to be faithful? The Hebrew word is *aman,* which means "to stand firm, to endure, long continuance, reliable, trusty."

I like the word "trusty," don't you? Faithfulness is not a flashy thing. It is not always an exciting thing. It can often be part of the drudgery of life. We do the same thing day after day as we mother in our homes. Life may seem monotonous. It may seem boring compared to the exciting life that others are leading outside the home. But, dear mother, be encouraged. You are fulfilling the most far-reaching and influential career in the nation!

Catherine Booth said, "I seek to make myself fit to be a mother, and being that in every sense, I shall be ready for any destiny God has for me." Be faithful in your home—your marriage, mothering, and all the little things you do in the "daily grind." This is your greatest training for life and eternity.

All your daily moments of faithfulness add up. They add up to a life of faithfulness. They add up to the reward of those wonderful words, *"Well done, thou good and faithful servant"* (Matthew 25:21). *Nancy*

Build and Benefit

My challenge for the day is Ephesians 4:29 NIV, *"Do not let any unwholesome talk come out of your mouths, but only what is helpful for building others up according to their needs, that it may benefit those who listen."* May all our words today do only two things—build and benefit. *Michelle*

- June 17 -

Rule Your Spirit

We read in Family Devotions this morning, *"He that is slow to anger is better than the mighty; and he that rules his spirit than he that takes a city"* (Proverbs 16:32).

I was inspiring some of my grandsons who were with us for Family Devotions that to rule their spirit is more powerful than capturing a city! But this truth applies to us mommies, too! When we rule our spirit, we show by example to our children how they can rule their spirit.

We wrote this Scripture out in BIG LETTERS and pinned it up on the wall so the children could memorize it. It is an important Scripture for us all to memorize. *Nancy*

Keep Practicing

How did the "building and benefitting" words go yesterday?

I found myself pulling out my "I Love Motherhood" and "I Love My Husband" bracelets to help me remember my challenge for the day.

It is more of a lifelong challenge than a day's challenge, but a goal worth practicing. I am sure that over time "building and benefiting" words will become the norm. Keep up the great job. *Michelle*

- June 18 -

A Picture of God's Love

"As I hold this baby in my arms,
I'm like a picture of You,
To nurture with Your love
Is what You made me to do."

I love these lines from Serene's song, *El Shaddai*. As you nurture your baby and children, you reveal what God is like. What a privilege!

Embrace your maternal-ness. If you have no children to nurture, ask God to show you someone to whom you can show His compassion and nurturing heart. *Nancy*

Lean on Your Father

Today, I was impacted by Isaiah 59:1, *"Behold, the Lord's hand is not shortened, that it cannot save, nor His ear heavy, that it cannot hear."*

How I needed that reminder! It is good for us to face concerns in our lives so that we learn to lean on our Father. He is mighty in power and able to do so much more than we can even think or imagine. *Michelle*

- June 19 -

Houseful of Smiling Children

Psalm 113:9 says, *"He makes the barren woman to keep house and to be a joyful mother of children."* Joy is the testimony of motherhood.

But, what if you don't feel joyful? Smile anyway! It's amazing how your attitude will catch up with your facial expression!

When you put this book down, get up and smile at your children. Smile each time you look at them today. Not only will you begin to feel joyful, but you'll soon have a houseful of smiling children. *Nancy*

Opinion or Truth?

"Are you done yet?" "Don't you know what causes that?" "I could never have enough patience!" "What on earth does your husband do for a living?" "Haven't you ever heard of birth control?" Common questions. Popular opinions. They are not Truth!

The truth is that God opens and closes the womb, He says children are a blessing, He says children bring joy and happiness, and He loves to bring forth godly seed. When someone offers an opinion, you have an open opportunity to offer truth!

When my OB told me my uterus was getting worn out, I said, "Isn't the uterus the strongest muscle in the body?" "Yes," she replied. "Well, all muscles get stronger with use," I responded. She didn't agree, but it is always a wonderful opportunity to spread the truth about children, when you are offered an opinion. *Michelle*

- June 20 -

God Will Not Let Me Go!

One of the Scriptures we read at Family Devotions this morning was Proverbs 4:12: *"When thou runnest, thou shalt not stumble."* My husband asked, "What do you think this means?" Our six-year-old grandson, Vision, put up his hand. He is always the first to put up his hand for every question!

He immediately recited, "When my foot begins to slip, God will hold me with His grip"—a little couplet I taught him two years previously. I was glad he still remembered it. It comes from Psalm 94:18, *"When I said, my foot slippeth; Thy mercy, O LORD, held me up."* It's a good couplet to learn yourself and teach your children—a truth they will need throughout the years. *Nancy*

Answered Prayer

My beloved Persian went missing, and we fell into a state of shock and despair. It seemed impossible to find a cat that doesn't go outside and was likely hiding and terrified. We prayed, knowing only God could bring him home.

I went out in the quiet of night at 3.00 a.m. when my three-year-old woke me. This time, my cat weakly answered! Even in small things, God is gracious to us. *Michelle*

- June 21 -

Every Meal a Love Affair

"Make every meal into a love affair." This is my challenge for each meal I create. It is not a matter of putting a meal together, but making the table a place where everyone in the family loves to come.

Take joy in preparing your meals today, dear mother. Don't do it out of resignation, but out of revelation, knowing that every meal has the power to bless your family and to bring the presence of God to your home.

The full quote is from "Babette's Feast" by Isak Dinesen. "And indeed... this woman is now turning a dinner into a kind of love affair—into a love affair of the noble and romantic category in which one no longer distinguishes between bodily and spiritual appetite or satiety!"

Your table is a place to feed not only the body, but the soul and the spirit, as well. *Nancy*

I'm Needed

I had to rush off the phone with the comment, "I have to go—someone needs me!"

This exact scenario has often caused me aggravation. Now it gives me a deep sense of gratitude and purpose. It is precious to be needed by people that love me. It is an honor to spend my time tending to the needs of my beloved family. I am thankful. *Michelle*

Highest Honor

I talked to a young mother recently whose two children are now at school. I said to her, "Are you hoping to have another baby?"

"Oh no," she replied. I'm enjoying my freedom too much now that they are at school!" Why do mothers want freedom from their children? Isn't this our destiny? We have been given the incredible privilege to house within our womb an eternal soul that will live forever and prepare that child to do mighty works in this life. What could be more powerful?

Why do mothers want to do inconsequential things when they could be doing eternal things? Why do they want to spend their time on "lesser" things when they could be doing "greater" things? I think it is because they are brainwashed by the liberal media and humanistic values of this society. This was not the psyche of the women of old; it was their highest honor to bear children. *Nancy*

Deal Graciously

"Those who live by grace will deal graciously with others!" I love this quote from my minister! When we remember how much grace has been given to us, we can more freely offer it to others, especially to those we cherish so dearly. Let's not react poorly in the trying moments; let's react graciously in His strength. *Michelle*

- June 23 -

Stay with Your Flock

Zechariah 11:17 NASB says, *"Woe to the worthless shepherd who leaves the flock!"*

Although this rebuke was spoken to the shepherds of Israel, it also relates to us as shepherd mothers. The Great Shepherd does not want us to leave the little flock He gives to us. He doesn't give us children to give them to someone else to care for while we fulfill our own agenda.

He gives us the responsibility to tenderly care for them and watch over them. It is not only a charge from God, but an awesome privilege. *Nancy*

Keep On Keeping On

Parenting is challenging, and sometimes we can be too hard on ourselves! If you read through the book of Kings, you will see repeatedly that a king *"did right in the eyes of the Lord,"* yet when his son eventually gets the throne, he does *"evil in the eyes of the Lord."*

Even godly kings had sons that were disobedient. Keep doing your best, and pray that God will bless it and that He will draw your children unto Himself! *Michelle*

- June 24 -

Wholesome Food

Ezekiel 34:14-15 says, *"I will **feed** them in a **good** pasture... there shall they lie in a **good** fold, and in a **fat** pasture shall they feed... I will **feed** My flock... saith the Lord."*

The Good Shepherd feeds His flock with **good** food. He leads them to **green** pastures. Food is a very big part of shepherding. Shouldn't we be like the Good Shepherd and seek to feed our families nourishing food, too? This vision makes preparing meals exciting and worthwhile. *Nancy*

You Create the Atmosphere

I have been in beautiful homes with the finest of furnishings and decor, and yet found the atmosphere to be filled with stress, strife, or anger. Other times, I have been in the poorest of homes that lack adequate furnishings, and yet felt the atmosphere of sweetness, cheerfulness, love, and relaxation.

It does not matter what your home looks like as much as how your home feels. The atmosphere in a home is not created by the physical beauty of its belongings as much as by the emotional energy it holds.

As mothers, we are directly responsible for that atmosphere! We need to be pleasant, sweet, loving, and perseverant under trials in order to have an atmosphere that blesses all who enter. We are able to do this as we lean into God who loves to love through us. *Michelle*

All Day Long

Deuteronomy 33:12 says, *"And of Benjamin He said, the beloved of the Lord shall dwell in safety by Him; and the Lord shall cover him all the day long, and he shall dwell between His shoulders."*

Mt. Zion belonged to the tribe of Judah; but Mt. Moriah, the site of the temple and where Jesus was crucified, belonged to the tribe of Benjamin. As we stay close to Jesus Christ the crucified, we can claim this promise. As we trust in the spotless blood of Jesus, the Lamb who was slain from the foundation of the world, we will experience His safety and covering over us. And, it's not only for a few minutes. It's all day long! Praise His name! *Nancy*

I'm His World

Isn't it terrific to be loved? I had a really busy day full of errands, and every time I left the house my three-year-old said, "Mum, I come a yuuu!"

The days pass so fast, and they grow up. I am thankful that he still wants to be with me all the time. I'm honored to be his world. I hope you are somebody's world, too. *Michelle*

- June 26 -

Chiseling Character

What kind of atmosphere pervades your home? Is it a rich soil of encouragement where your children blossom into all God has created them to be?

S. D. Gordon writes, "The influence exerted by the mother is great beyond the power of our minds to think or of our words to tell. The making of the child's character is in the mother's hands to a degree that is nothing short of startling."

The words of wisdom you speak into your children while they are young will go with them throughout life. Proverbs 6:20-24 says, *"Forsake not the law (teaching) of thy mother... When thou goest, it shall lead thee; when thou sleepest, it shall keep thee; and when thou awakest, it shall talk with thee. For the commandment is a lamp; and the law (teaching) is light; and reproofs of instruction are the way of life."* Your teaching and mothering continues into adulthood. *Nancy*

Feed Encouragement

Husbands and children thrive on encouragement. Feed it to them! *Michelle*

- June 27 -

Blessed Memories

Your children will remember the atmosphere of your home more than anything else. Create an atmosphere for your husband and children that will be a delight to savor and remember.

Can I quote D. S. Gordon again? "The atmosphere of the home is breathed in by the child, and exerts an influence in his training more than all other things put together. The child receives more by unconscious absorption than in any other way. The spirit of the home then is the one thing on which the keen mind and earnest heart of the father and mother will center most."

Create a love-filled home today. *Nancy*

Better Things to Do

Sure, we can find plenty to complain about, but whatever for? Life is too short, and we have much better things to do with our time. Enjoy every drop of your life today. You won't get another day just like today, so make the most of it! Look for the excellent and praiseworthy parts of today. And don't forget the power of prayer. *Michelle*

You Are What You Think

The Bible gets it right every time. Before science ever discloses a truth, God has already established it. Here's another maxim that God established from the beginning, *"For as he thinketh in his heart, so is he"* (Proverbs 23). You can't get away from it. What you think is how you live.

Are your thoughts full of self-pity? Don't expect to rise up out of your pit. Are your thoughts filled with selfishness and how everything should revolve around you? Expect to stay miserable. Do you harbor anger and bitterness in your heart toward your husband or anyone else? You are on the way to self-destruction.

There's only one way out. Change your thought patterns. Change them to what God says about you. Meditate in God's Word and make it your confession. Think of how to make your husband and children happy. Think love. Think forgiveness. Think blessing. Think joy. Think peace. Think God's thoughts, and you are on the way to life and victory. *Nancy*

Give Lots of Love Today

Love is so powerful. Well, of course it is, because God is love. Have fun loving today. Marvel at its power and experience it. *Michelle*

Yes, I can!

Because my God is Omnificent (all-creating), the One who created the world and every intricate part of my body, can I not trust Him with every aspect of my physical body?

Because my God is Omnipotent (all-powerful), can I not trust Him to sovereignly rule my life rather than putting my trust in mere man?

Because my God is Omniscient (all-wise and all-knowing), can I not trust Him to teach me and lead me in His paths?

Because my God is Omnipresent (all-present God), can I not trust Him to be with me in my home and in all situations?

Because my God is Omnibenevolent (all-good and all-loving), can I not trust Him, knowing that even when I am going through difficult times, and everything looks impossible that He is working it out for good? Yes, I can! *Nancy*

Why not Build?

Are you building up? Or tearing down? Both take the same amount of energy, so why not build? *Michelle*

- June 30 -

God is Great from A to Z

My God is so great that He cannot be confined to one name or even one attribute. Worship Him with me today, for He is Almighty, Burden-Bearer, Comforter, Deliverer, Everlasting Father, Faithful, Glorious, Helper, I AM THAT I AM, Just, Kind, Loving, Merciful, Nurturer, Omnipotent, Patient, Quietude, Ruler, Sovereign, Trustworthy, Unchangeable, Victorious, Wisdom, eXaminer of my heart, Yearner over His children, and Zealous.

Take time to teach your children the character of God. Take one of these attributes each day, then talk about it with your children and ask them to tell you how they understand that particular aspect of God. Together, praise and honor God for who He is. It will take a month or more to go through them. *Nancy*

Parents in Love

Date nights or some form of couple time is very important to a marriage. When I was getting ready to go out with Cam, our seven-year-old daughter, Jilissa, smiled at me and said, "I will leave you alone so you can get ready for your date with Dad." She was so excited about it!

Children love to see their parents in love and spending time together! *Michelle*

- July 1 -

Abundantly Encourage

I blew it! One little negative word, and it knocks out loads of encouraging words! Back to repenting again! I find now, and in all my experience of raising children, that one negative word can enter into my husband or my children and affect them detrimentally; whereas, it takes many encouraging words for them to really feel encouraged. Have you noticed this, too?

We have to constantly, daily, and abundantly pour on encouraging words. *Nancy*

Ripple Effects

Our four-year-old son was watching a DVD with most of the family when he asked his dad, "Is that the Momma?"

"Yes, that's the Momma," Daddy answered.

Contentedly, Drayden snuggled down with a sigh and passionately exclaimed, "I love all mommas!"

I heard this from the kitchen, and had to come over and see the boy who put such a big smile on my face!

Remember, Momma, you are deeply loved. Other children look at you as you mother your children, and they feel all warm and fuzzy inside—the ripple effects of motherhood. I love them. *Michelle*

- July 2 -

Sacred Humdrum

Everything is sacred when God is in it. In Acts 6:1-3 the disciples are told to find men *"full of the Holy Spirit and wisdom"* to look after tables and widows.

We must be filled with the Holy Spirit to do the menial tasks in our home as much as someone preaching in the pulpit! God is with you as you change diapers, clean toilets, and prepare meals as much as someone in fulltime work for God!

Ask God to fill you with His Holy Spirit for every mundane task, and your home will be filled with the fragrance of the Lord. *Nancy*

Awesome Honor

What a privilege to be a mother and share with God in creating life. It truly is an awesome and amazing honor to be entrusted with another life to raise for God, even when the going gets tough! To realize that we are bestowed the honor at all, is absolutely incredible. Savor it today and always. Even in the sorrow of loss, we are still blessed to have conceived. *Michelle*

A Broken Attitude

As we seek to drive out evil from our homes, we must guard against the media! This takes constant vigil! There are Christians who compromise with the devil by watching lustful scenes on their TV screen, thereby allowing the spirit of fornication and adultery to enter their home. Jeremiah 23:9-10 tells us his attitude toward adultery—his heart was broken within him! Is this the kind of attitude that we have? *Nancy*

The Ultimate Career

"The homemaker has the ultimate career. All other careers exist for one purpose only—and that is to support the ultimate career " (C.S. Lewis).

Being a homemaker truly is the ultimate career, the ultimate adventure, the ultimate lifestyle, and the ultimate experience. Embrace it for all of its wonderfulness! Even if you are not presently a fulltime homemaker, it is still your most ultimate career, above any other one. It may rarely offer an actual paycheck, as other careers may, but the eternal rewards, and even the earthly joys, are immeasurable!

I love my ultimate career! *Michelle*

- July 4 -

It's Your Expression

"Beauty does not lie in the face. It lies in the harmony between man and his industry. Beauty is expression. When I paint a mother, I try to render her beautiful by the mere look she gives her child." (Jean Millet).

Isn't that so true? I don't think there is anything more beautiful than a mother looking with adoration at her baby. The plainest mother is beautiful when she looks lovingly at her child. It truly is the expression of our face that is beautiful to the beholder. It is our expression that comes from within that makes a woman beautiful or otherwise. May the expression on our face make us look beautiful to our husband and children. *Nancy*

We Get Things Done!

I'm a homemaker! It is the most accomplished title available to women! It is far more powerful than my degree. As housewives, we multitask and get things done! We are not quitters, as there is no shortage of work. We clean, cook, mend, nurture, care for the needs of the home and the family, and we know how to work around all kinds of disruptions! We are financial wizards, hairdressers, fashion designers, chefs, physicians, personal trainers, teachers, organizers, managers, nutritionists, counselors, chauffeurs, motivational speakers, coaches, librarians, singers, dancers, lawyers, judges, hostesses, lovers, creators, writers, maids, laundresses, comedians, mechanics, bakers, gardeners, and so much more! We are world changers! That's right! Just doing our job as homemakers! *Michelle*

You Are Royalty

"Ye are the children of the Lord your God" (Deuteronomy 14:1).
What does this mean? I am a redeemed, blood-bought child of the
King of the universe. Not any king, but the King of kings. I am
royalty. You are royalty. Therefore we should live like royalty. The
Knox translation says, *"Learn to carry yourselves as the children of
the Lord your God."*

Do you speak like royalty—like a daughter of the King of kings? Do
you walk like a daughter of royalty? Do you dress like a daughter of
the King of kings? That means modestly, but also beautifully. You
won't see a princess in drab, dreary clothes. Do you live in every way
like a daughter of the King? Are you teaching your daughters to carry
themselves and walk as daughters of the King? Acknowledge who you
are and live accordingly. *Nancy*

Powerful Work

Being a wife and mother within the home is powerful. My Bible's
notes on Proverbs 31 say, "The noble wife's accomplishments (her
tangible contributions to the household) empower her husband to lead
the nation in righteousness and justice."

Your work is powerful indeed, positively impacting your husband,
your children and the next generation. *Michelle*

- July 6 -

Nation-Impacting Career

Isaiah 61:9 NASB is another promise to pray and believe for our children, *"Their offspring will be known among the nations, and their descendants in the midst of the peoples. All who see them will recognize them because they are the offspring whom the Lord has blessed."*

You may think you are hidden in your home as you quietly and faithfully nurture and teach your children in the ways of God, but you are preparing them to impact nations. You have a nation-impacting career. *Nancy*

Bite Your Tongue

It's easy to see the negative and let it consume the atmosphere of our home. However, when we choose to see the positive, praise flows freely from our lips, and joy fills our homes. A worthy goal is to speak on whatever is praiseworthy, and as much as possible, bite your tongue on the rest.

This is a path to a happy, loving atmosphere in the home. *Michelle*

- July 7 -

The Tone of Your Voice

We are reminded in Ephesians 4:32 to *"Be kind one to another, tenderhearted, forgiving one another."* Did you know that this means being kind to your husband and children first? And it's even more than WHAT we say; it's HOW we say it. An unknown writer encourages us...

> *It is not so much what you say,*
> *As the manner in which you say it;*
> *It is not so much the language you use*
> *As the tones you use to convey it.*
> *For words come from the mind*
> *And grow by study and art;*
> *But tones leap forth from the inner self*
> *And reveal the state of the heart.*

Nancy

No Other Place

Your work of mothering is mighty. There is no other place that is better for you to be than right where the Lord has you. He will not leave you nor forsake you! Do not cave into lies that tell you otherwise. Take great pride and joy in your mighty work, your mighty place, and your mighty position! *Michelle*

- July 8 -

Give What You Have

A man who was lame from birth sat at the temple gate to beg. When he saw Peter and John going into the temple for the 3.00 p.m. prayer meeting, he asked for money. Peter answered, *"Silver and gold have I none; but such as I have give I thee: In the name of Jesus Christ of Nazareth rise up and walk"* (Acts 3:6).

I am challenged. I often think that "when I have money," I will be able to help certain ministries and do greater things for God. But the early disciples didn't have silver and gold, and they turned the world upside down! They gave what they had—the life-giving power of God residing in them through the infilling of the Holy Spirit.

Let's forget about what we don't have, and give what we do have—the power of God residing in us to bless others' lives. *Nancy*

More Fit After Children

Who says having many pregnancies ruins your body? I have had 16 pregnancies, 11 of them full term, and am still within 10 pounds of my teenage weight! In addition, I am more fit now, at 42, than I ever was in my twenties or teens. If it is true for me, it can be true for you. I am not special and was never athletic in my youth. *Michelle*

- July 9 -

The Dwelling God

I love the way God relates to our lives. God is a God of the home. He lives in a home (the Bible tells us that it is somewhere in the "north"). Because He lives in a home, He wants His people to live in a home, too. The same Hebrew word that speaks of God's habitation is used to describe our home or an animal's home.

God wants us to have a retreat from the storms of the world, a shelter from the elements, and a place in which to settle. God is a "dwelling" God. He wants to dwell in my life and your life (Colossians 1:27). He wants to dwell in my home and your home and our corporate family life (II Corinthians 6:16). He wants to dwell in His body, the church (Ephesians 1:23).

Is He resting and comfortable in your home? *Nancy*

Sighing Will Flee

I was convicted about sighing the other day. Isaiah 35:10 says, *"They shall obtain joy and gladness, and sorrow and sighing shall flee away."*

May all the sighs that escape our lips be those of contentment! Sighs of discontent and frustration do us no good, but sighs filled with contentment are life-giving and pleasing to God! *Michelle*

- July 10 -

Lead Me to the Rock

The psalmist cried, *"When my heart is overwhelmed: lead me to the rock that is higher than I"* (Psalm 61:2). It's hard to lift up your head when you feel overwhelmed, isn't it? This "weighed down" state can lead you to depression, worry, self-pity, or to seek refuge in human resources.

But the answer is to allow God to lead you to **Him**. He is the Rock. He is dependable and will not let you down. He is higher than your circumstances. His ways are higher than your depressing thoughts. Only in Him will you find true refuge. *Nancy*

Stepping Stone to Success

Do you feel as though you are failing? Me, too! The very fact that we are aware of our failing means we are exactly where we need to be to change things and gain victory. Recognition is the first step towards improvement.

Don't be discouraged at knowing you have failed; be encouraged. At least you recognize it and are ready to call upon the Lord for your victory. Failure = opportunity = growth = victory! Love the process and the progress! *Michelle*

Flourish in Your Home

Are you wilting in your home today? Or, perhaps you are just making it through. What about flourishing? Is this possible? Yes, this is God's purpose for you.

I love the New Living Translation of Psalm 128:3-4, *"Your wife will be like a fruitful vine, FLOURISHING WITHIN YOUR HOME. And look at all those children! There they sit around your table as vigorous and healthy as young olive trees. That is the Lord's reward for those who fear Him."*

God wants you to flourish and bloom. And, where does He want you to flourish? In your home. Dear mother, get out of survival mode into thriving mode. Dream of ways to flourish and soon you will be flourishing on every hand. *Nancy*

God is Mighty for you

Do you long to see God's power in your life today? *"For the eyes of the Lord run to and fro throughout the whole earth, to show Himself strong in the behalf of them whose heart is perfect toward Him"* (II Chronicles 16:9).

He delights to show His mighty power to you! He has shown me His might time and again when I have prayed this Scripture. *Michelle*

I Am an Up-Builder

II Corinthians 12:19 says, *"We do all things, dearly beloved, for your edifying."* The NASB reads, *"All for your UPBUILDING, beloved."* Everything Paul wrote and spoke was for the up-building of the saints.

I want this to be my vision, too, don't you? Will everything I say to my husband today build him up and make him feel as though he is the most amazing man in the universe? Will everything I say to each of my children today build them up so they will be stronger in their spirit and in truth?

What about you? *Nancy*

Don't Act Like a Victim

Do you feel "victimized" in an area of your life today? Are you battling self-pity? Jesus Christ was the ultimate victim and had every reason to wallow in self-pity. Yet, He never behaved as a victim, and He continued to pour Himself out for others.

With Christ as our strength, no matter what we face, we can do the same! *Michelle*

- July 13 -

Is God Welcome?

Did you know that God wants to walk with you and fellowship with you in your home? Genesis 3:8 says, *"They heard the voice of the Lord God walking in the garden in the cool of the day."*

This was the Garden of Eden, the first home, the prototype of all homes to come. God loves to walk in gardens, and in homes. He wants to walk in your home, too.

Leviticus 26:12 says, *"I will also **walk among you** and be your God, and you shall be My people."* Read also Jeremiah 31:1, Ezekiel 37:27 and II Corinthians 6:16. Does God have the freedom to walk in every room in your home? *Nancy*

A Love-Filled Day

God is love and His love endures forever. I am not only amazed by His love, but overwhelmed with the many opportunities we have to love and minister to others, both within and outside of the home. What a privilege we have to show His love to all those in our lives! And what brings more joy than love? Have a day full of love! *Michelle*

- July 14 -

You Are Not Forgotten

Isaiah 49:15-16 says, *"Can a woman forget her sucking child, that she should not have compassion on the son of her womb? Yea, they may forget, yet will I not forget thee. Behold, I have graven thee upon the palms of my hands; **thy walls are continually before me**."*

Do you sometimes think that you are all on your own as you mother your little ones in your home? Maybe you think that even God has forgotten you! Don't listen to these lies. God is watching over the walls of your home. His eyes do not leave your home. He sees you cooking, changing diapers, washing dishes, and doing laundry—and He is pleased. *Nancy*

Smarten Up

I think that we are told to serve others for our own good more than the good of others! This morning my focus was on myself, a mixture of self-pity and selfishness. My mood was foul, and the atmosphere of the entire home was suffering. This is the wisdom of the world. To look out for #1, and "take care of yourself, because nobody else will" is complete foolishness to God. Centering on my own needs created a miserable mood.

God's wisdom is to lose myself in service to God and to others. This creates joy! It's time for me to smarten up, get my eyes off myself, keep my eyes on Christ, and serve others humbly. Who will be blessed? Me! I will enjoy a sweet and beautiful atmosphere in the home. You will, too. *Michelle*

- July 15 -

We Become What We Say

Isaiah 3:8 NASB says, *"Jerusalem has stumbled and fallen because their **speech** and their **actions** are against the Lord."*

So often we confess the opposite of what God says, don't we? When we speak words of doubt, despair, and defeat, we speak against the Lord because He is our God of Deliverance. When we confess fear, not literal fear, but the fear of what MIGHT HAPPEN, we speak against God because fear is the opposite of faith. When we say, "Can God provide?" we speak against God, because He is Jehovah Jireh.

Do you notice that *"speech"* comes before *"actions"*? We become what we say! *Nancy*

Believe the Best

When someone holds you in high regard, don't you desire to be the person they think you are? You are motivated to be a better person, because they believe in you, and you don't want to let them down.

We are all keenly aware of our faults, and the faults of others, but focusing on them only stunts our growth. Rather, see and believe the best in your husband, your children, and others. *Michelle*

- July 16 -

The Right Confession

Rather than confessing *"Can God prepare a table in the wilderness?"* (how often we confess these doubting words), why don't we confess, *"Is anything too hard for the Lord?"* (Psalm 78:19 and Genesis 18:14)? Our confession exposes our understanding of God, doesn't it? And, it displeases God when we do not believe and trust Him. Verse 21 says, *"Therefore the Lord heard this, and was wroth... and anger also came up against Israel."*

If we know that God is Omnipotent and nothing is too hard for Him, we will surely have a positive confession. May we habitually confess the character of God rather than our puny unbelief. *Nancy*

Fresh Courage

> *"Ye fearful saints, fresh courage take;*
> *The clouds ye so much dread,*
> *Are big with mercy and shall break,*
> *In blessings on your head."*

Lyrics from a hymn by William Cowper—aren't they wonderful? And so true! *"All things work together for good to them that love God"* (Romans 8:28). Face today with fresh courage! *Michelle*

Don't You Love Work?

I am sure I don't have to remind you that mothering is hard work! It's how it's meant to be. When God put Adam and Eve in the garden home, He gave them work to do—and that was before the fall of man.

Don't complain that your mothering career takes work! Work is a blessing. Work is therapeutic. Work releases creativity. God told the first couple to "dress" the garden. The word in the Hebrew is *avad* and means to "work until weary, to be fatigued."

God reiterates the same theme in the New Testament in I Timothy 5:10 where He tells us that feeding and raising children is a *"good work."* The Greek word is *ergon* and means, "work that is not accomplished by a single act but by accumulated labor and continued work."

That sounds like daily mothering, doesn't it? Rejoice as you work. Sing while you work. You are in the perfect will of God. *Nancy*

Blessed Indeed

What a privilege to be able to stay home, raise children, and build family relationships. I am so glad that I don't have to sell my time today for a paycheck. I am a woman most blessed indeed. This is truly living in my books. *Michelle*

- July 18 -

God Is Good

God cannot do anything but good, because He is inherently good. This is His nature. We look out upon the world and see so much evil and suffering, but in it all, God is still good. We have evil in the world, but it does not change God's goodness. We go through difficult and traumatic times, but again, it does not change God's goodness. God is Sovereign and working all things out for good.

Joseph was torn away from his family as a young teen and taken to a foreign country. He was put in prison and faced disappointment after disappointment. But God was working it out for good.

When the time came to be reconciled to his brothers, he confessed, *"But as for you, ye thought evil against me; **but God meant it unto good**, to bring to pass, as it is this day, to save much people alive"* (Genesis 45:7-8 and 50:20).

God is working everything in your life for good, too. Trust Him, and acknowledge His goodness. *Nancy*

Goodbye Selfishness

Today I must run in many directions for many different family members. It is the perfect antidote for self-centeredness. Thank you, Lord, for having a family to care for. It keeps me busy, and selfishness becomes less of a battle in my life as I serve my precious eleven children. Happy serving today! *Michelle*

See What God Can Do!

I was thinking this morning that stuff does not satisfy! Some mothers think that they could never manage on one income. But they will never know until they take that scary step of faith and see what God can do. God waits to show His faithfulness to us, but often we don't give Him a chance.

It's amazing how much cheaper you can live when you are home. When you only shop once a week, or once every two weeks, you save hundreds of dollars. The less you go to shops, the less you spend. You can cook everything from scratch, using wholesome, non-packaged foods. You can grow a garden and eat fresh, non-sprayed vegetables. You save on gas and clothes. And you are with your precious children. You are doubly-blessed. *Nancy*

Show Hospitality

Today, I feel honored to show hospitality. Thank you, Lord, for having something to share, for folks that want to come over and spend time with us, for having schedules to allow for it, and for having an opportunity to grow a relationship. I must not take it for granted. Have a hospitable day! *Michelle*

Wonder and Awe

I love the lines of Sara Teasdale: "Children's faces looking up, Holding wonder like a cup." "Wonder" is an emotion God has given to us, firstly, in relation to Him. He is called "Wonderful" (Isaiah 9:6). The word is *pele* and literally means, "a wonder, a marvel." God cannot be fathomed. He is mysterious (Job 11:7-10). Judges 13:18 says His name is *"secret."* God should be our greatest awe as we continually receive new glimpses and understanding of Him and His amazing creation.

Do we awake each morning filled with wonder and expectation of what God will do and show us? Or have the stresses and burdens of life dimmed this wonder? Perhaps excessive media and iphones, etc., have blurred our brains from seeing the wonder and expectation in life. A book I am reading currently talks about a delightful clockmaker who "had never grown up and things still amazed him."

May you and I be those who keep being amazed! Ask God to renew in you the delight of wonder. Together, with your children, daily look for God and His wonders, not only in the big things of life, but also the tiny little things. Live in the expectation of wonder today. *Nancy*

The Shortest Chapter

The shortest chapter of life is that of childhood. The adult chapter can typically last at least five times longer. Savor every second you have to watch your child move through this extra-special time. Love every second of it. *Michelle*

Quintessentially Feminine

Why do we tend to be more like society than to embrace what God created us to be? I think it is because the devil seeks to distort God's original intention. The more we embrace our femininity, our motherliness, and our life-giving power, the more we reveal to the world the purpose and plan of God for women.

What does it mean to you to be a female? I think of these words— femininity, womanliness, conception, wombing, life-giving, mothering, nurturing, nesting, nourishing, feeding, succoring, embracing, enriching, encouraging, helping, inspiring, comforting, strengthening, forgiving, and self-sacrificing.

As you embrace this beautiful picture of womanhood, you not only nurture your family, but you build a nation! *Nancy*

Poured Out

"Yea, and if I be offered upon the sacrifice and service of your faith, I joy, and rejoice with you all" (Philippians 2:17).

Are you being poured out? When we are poured out, we are refilled by the power of the Spirit. We are emptied for the cause of Christ as we minister to our sweet families, and we rejoice when they come to faith. *Michelle*

- July 22 -

Take Your Family to Church

Terry Johnson writes, "The most important single commitment you have to make to ensure your family's spiritual well-being is to regular, consistent attendance at public worship."

I totally agree. Committing to a church fellowship, whether large or small, is a very important part of establishing a godly family. God's Word confirms the same in Hebrews 10: 25, *"Not forsaking the assembling of ourselves together, as the manner of some is; but exhorting one another: and so much the more, as ye see the day approaching."*

Whether you worship on Saturday or Sunday, be committed to the fellowship of the saints. Not haphazardly, but regularly. You are establishing an ordained biblical principle that must carry on from generation to generation. If you let it go, what will the next generation do? *Nancy*

God's Always Right!

I love it when modern day studies prove what God has already written in His word. A study on increasing happiness lists five points: helping others, expressing gratitude, forgiving, looking for the positive, and making religious practice a habit. All of these keys to happiness are given to us in the Bible. We need no other advice! *Michelle*

Stop Dreaming, Start Doing

The affirmation I repeat often is, "Things don't just happen. You have to make them happen!"

It's true. You can get great ideas and visions. You can dream about them for weeks, but until you actually do something, nothing happens. I am always dreaming up new ideas, but I don't only dream. I like to make them happen.

Are you dreaming of organizing your house? Stop dreaming and start cleaning. Start in one room and organize it before you go onto the next. Is your laundry piling high? Get stuck into it, and don't stop until it is completed! Are you wondering how to get a meal on the table in the evening? Put some meat and veggies in the crockpot in the morning and they'll be cooked and waiting for you. *Nancy*

Never Too Late to Make Amends

I caught myself correcting rudeness in one of my children while using a very rude tone of voice myself! I realized it afterwards, but did not immediately make amends. Sometimes it amazes me that God trusts me to raise all these people!

Well, without all my faults, I wouldn't need Him so much. Now, I will apologize at breakfast tomorrow. It's never too late to fix things up! *Michelle*

- July 24 -

A Visit from God!

What was Mary's reaction when she conceived the Christ child by the power of the Holy Spirit? How could it work out in her situation? It would bring her shame, persecution, and ridicule. She was poor. How would she provide for this child? Yet she rejoiced.

"And Mary said, My soul doth magnify the Lord, and my spirit hath rejoiced in God my Savior" (Luke 1:46-47).

What is your response when you conceive? Do you rejoice in the amazement that an eternal soul who will bear the image of God is growing inside you?

Did you know that when you conceive, you are *"visited"* by God? What could be more awesome than a visitation of God? Genesis 21:1-2 says, *"The Lord visited Sarah... for Sarah conceived, and bare Abraham a son."* Again it says in I Samuel 2:21, *"And the Lord visited Hannah, so that she conceived, and bare three sons and two daughters."* Doesn't a "visitation" call for rejoicing? *Nancy*

Show Mercy

Matthew 5:7 says, *"Blessed are the merciful: for they shall obtain mercy."* What mercy shall we receive if we are critical, vindictive, avenging, or condemning? How will it damage our testimony? Showing mercy allows us to imitate God and brings honor and respect to our relationships. It also keeps our heart soft and humble, rather than hard or proud. *Michelle*

Don't Feel Sorry for Me

An *Above Rubies* reader, Rachel Malcolm, inspired by the ministry of *Above Rubies*, wrote to me: "I am home every day with my children. We have a limited budget and rarely go on trips or out for dinner. I don't own a washing machine, and I don't have running water. But don't feel sorry for me, because I am free!

I am free from debt, depression, and disease. I am free to jump on the trampoline or have a tea party with my children. I am free to teach them right from wrong, free to teach them how to read, free to explore the wonders of creation with them. I am free to worship God and read His Word. I am free to work in my garden and enjoy the labor of my hands. I am free to choose whether to be thankful or feel sorry for myself; and I am free to make that choice every day."

You are free too. Make the right choice. *Nancy*

Pray and Smile

Are you living on a prayer? Isn't that the ticket to living in joy and peace? Since faith believes in things hoped for and not seen, a prayer lifted gives us faith that God will manage the rest. No need to worry or become fearful once everything is lifted to God. You can smile instead. Isn't it amazing how prayer and a smile can have such positive results in our mothering? I really should try it more! *Michelle*

- July 26 -

Ending Future Dynasties

When a couple refuses to have children or voluntarily stops having children (please note that I wrote "voluntarily," as my heart grieves with those who are unable to conceive), they deprive grandparents of their *"crowns"* and fathers of their *"glory."* They also deprive the nation and future generations of their *"glory."* They also deprive God of His army (Psalm 127:5 and Zechariah 9:13).

Every child that is cut off is not only one child that is stopped, but also a future dynasty! (Proverbs 17:6 and Hosea 9:11) *Nancy*

Opportunities for Growth

If we let failure bring us down, it wins twice! Failing keeps us humble, keeps us learning, and keeps us leaning on God—all necessary for our ultimate success.

Our failures are only opportunities for further improvement and growth. We can move forward in victory. *Michelle*

A Mother's Creed

I am not languishing. I am not deceived. I have a vision. I know who I am and who God created me to be. I know my purpose. I am walking in the perfect will of God. I know it's not easy, but I've counted the cost. My goal is set. How could my career be easy when I am influencing a nation for God, generations to come—and eternity?

How can it be easy when I am destroying the plans of the devil? Such is the power of my God-mandated career, the highest calling ever given to women—motherhood. I have embraced my calling. I am not intimidated by my antagonists. I will not be moved. My heart is fixed.

I may be hidden in my home, but look out world! I am sharpening my arrows. I am getting them ready to shoot forth and destroy the adversary. In the power and anointing of God, I am advancing God's Kingdom. *Nancy*

Double Blessing

Would you like to have more rest? How about more delight? Proverbs 29:17 says, *"Correct thy son, and he shall give thee **rest**; yea, he shall give **delight** unto thy soul."*

All the effort we exert in child training will bless us with both rest and delight! A double blessing! This is terrific motivation to stay the course, isn't it? *Michelle*

Soft and Soothing

Proverbs 15:4 Amplified says, *"A gentle tongue (with its healing power) is a tree of life, but willful contrariness in it breaks down the spirit."* Soft and soothing words heal hurts, restore estrangements in your marriage relationship, and diffuse arguments.

Sharp words make tempers hot, whereas gentle words turn away anger. Practice speaking gentle words today. They are incredibly powerful! *Nancy*

We Make Them Proud

I must say that the most refreshing thing I read today was Proverbs 17:6b NIV, *"Parents are the pride of their children."* Sometimes, in the short term, it can feel quite the opposite. We need the reminder. Be encouraged in your parenting today! *Michelle*

- July 29 -

More Power

How are the *"gentle"* words going in your home? Are they blessing your marriage? I read this morning, *"Sweetness of speech increases persuasiveness"* (Proverbs 16:21 NASB).

You will have more power in influencing your husband by speaking sweet words to him than by arguing. The picture of the bride in Song of Solomon 4:11 is of honey dripping from her mouth.

What does honey taste like? Sweet! That's right. Keep the sweet words dripping from your mouth. *Nancy*

Proper Focus

"Some people are always grumbling because roses have thorns; I am thankful that thorns have roses."

I love this quote. It offers one key to having a cheerful heart—the proper focus. There are many ways to look at the same thing. God's Word reminds us to choose the positive, praiseworthy way! *Michelle*

- July 30 -

Best Wrinkle Remover

Would you like to hear about a great wrinkle remover? I've found the best! Let me share it with you.

*"Christ also loved the church, and gave Himself for it; that He might sanctify and cleanse it with the washing of water by the Word, that He might present it to Himself a glorious church, **not having spot, or wrinkle or any such thing**, but that it should be holy and without blemish"* (Ephesians 5:25-27).

The best wrinkle remover is the Word of God. For faster results, apply it twice a day! Nancy

A Great Strategy

Want to have a great day today? Because I am operating on not enough sleep this morning, I had to come up with a workable plan. My strategy is to consciously build up and bless every single person I have contact with today, focusing on their strengths and positive character qualities. It has already helped me to feel amazing. May it help you, too. *Michelle*

- July 31 -

Removes Blemishes, Too!

Did you apply your wrinkle remover this morning? Ephesians 5:27 tells us that the Word of God is not only a wrinkle remover, but a spot cleaner and blemish remover! We certainly can't do without our daily applications for the beauty that God wants to work in our lives. *Nancy*

Why Do I Forget?

I can be so forgetful. I forget little things, like where I left something, but I also forget big things, like how omnipotent God is!

Both yesterday and today, the Lord swiftly answered prayer for me, despite my doubts after praying. I didn't doubt that He heard me. I only had doubts that things would turn out the way I wanted them to. I seem to forget that God is Sovereign and not even a hair can fall from my head without His knowledge.

So why do I worry and fret? I forget! I forget how big, how awesome, and how in control of all things HE is—even of my hair. That leaves no room for fret, doubt, discouragement, or complaining. It only leaves room for peace and trust. *Michelle*

- August 1 -

Pass On the Trade

Many young women today have no clue about cooking. There's no other reason than that their mothers have not passed on to them this important trade. Cooking nutritious and aroma-filled meals and sitting around the table together to enjoy them is a tradition that must continue down the generations!

My granddaughter, Rashida has just turned 16 years. She is such a blessing in her home of 10 children and cooks most of the meals. But she didn't start recently. She has been cooking for the family from a little child.

Every year that my father came to visit us from New Zealand, Rashida would cook a special meal for her great-granddad. She was only seven years old when she prepared this feast—roast turkey with coos coos stuffing (including sundried tomatoes, cashews, pine nuts, figs and raisins); marinated grape leaves stuffed with lebani, placed in a bowl with figs, dates, and black and green olives; mashed potatoes and gravy; salad with homemade dressings (almondaise and Green Greek dressing) and tamarind date chutney. Yes, there was dessert, too—ginger steamed pudding and raw nut balls.

If a seven-year-old can do it, you can, too. Go for it. *Nancy*

No Room for Complaining

Today, I will be a smiling servant! That means there will be no room for complaining in my home. *Michelle*

All Around the World

It is a joy, when traveling, to join with families around the world as they conduct Family Devotions with their children.

In Scotland, we stayed with a Polish family where we all prayed and heartily sang hymns together.

In England, we enjoyed Family Devotions with a young couple with two little boys.

In Holland, we joined a young family who are reading through the Old Testament at breakfast time and were up to Ezekiel. They then read a chapter from the New Testament at evening devotions. After reading, they prayed in Dutch, we prayed in English, and we all sang together.

You can tell your children when you have Family Devotions that they are joining with other families all around the world. *Nancy*

Shine Brightly

You are ultimately all that you can control and use to impact the world, so make sure you are drawing others in with your infectious energy and attitude. People will want what you have—the Lord, a strong marriage, happy children—when they see evidence of these things positively working in your own life, so let your life shine brightly! *Michelle*

- August 3 -

Reclaim the Nation

Motherhood is the highest career of all careers in the nation. Without motherhood the nation will die. Without godly mothers in the home, the nation fails. Without godly mothers in the home, reading God's Word to their children from the time they are born, Christianity dies. The enemy knows this fact and that is why he woos mothers out of the home. He knows that if he can steal the children from Christian families, he wins the battle.

Don't be asleep to the enemy's tactics. Be on the offensive. Embrace your career of motherhood with all your heart. If you don't love motherhood at this stage, start confessing that you love it. You'll be amazed at how you will change when you change your confession.

Begin every day by confessing aloud, "I LOVE MOTHERHOOD!" Keep saying it until it is part of you. Rise up in the power and anointing of motherhood, build a strong marriage and home, and take up the challenge to raise godly sons and daughters who will not be influenced by this world system. In doing so, you will be part of reclaiming your nation for God. *Nancy*

Radiate Love

Are you making the most of your circumstances today? Are you redeeming the time and loving on your husband and children? I want to radiate love and encouragement today, don't you? I want to make life better for all those around me, for there will never be another today. *Michelle*

- August 4 -

The Star of the Show

There is nothing more beautiful than a baby, is there? A baby makes everyone smile. Sometime back, my daughter Serene and I were doing our grocery shopping together. She was carrying baby Breeze (two months old) in her arms. Nearly everyone stopped to look at the baby or talk to her.

"I'm the star of the show," Serene commented, "just because I'm carrying a baby!"

When I am out shopping I often look around for babies. I never see very many. Wouldn't it be wonderful to see mothers and babies everywhere? This is the blessing of the nation. *Nancy*

What's Right?

A helpful quote that I have used many times over the years is, "Don't ask yourself what is wrong with it, ask yourself what is RIGHT with it!" This has often helped our family keep things in their proper perspective. It can also be applied when we assess how we are communicating. Have a honey-filled day. *Michelle*

A Resting Place

Did you know that God's Word calls your home a resting place? Isn't that a delightful name? But God means what He says in His Word. He doesn't want inside pressures or outside evil influences to spoil your resting place. Proverbs 24:15 says, *"Lay not wait, O wicked man, against the dwelling of the righteous, spoil not his resting place."*

Guard your resting place. Deal with every situation that spoils the rest in your home. Don't let them fester and grow bigger. Resist all outside evil influences. Take time to create order and peace in your home. Make it what God wants it to be—a "resting place." *Nancy*

Trails Worth Following

As a mother, I spend a lot of time tidying "trails" that others leave behind. As I pondered this, I realized that we all leave trails—the question is where do our trails lead? My older children are leaving a trail for their siblings to follow, and I challenge them to make their trail worth following.

Is my "trail" worth following? Is yours? *Michelle*

- August 6 -

Pray for Coming Generations

Each morning, my husband and I not only pray for our children and grandchildren, but for the generations to come, that they will continue to walk in the ways of the Lord and be mighty in the land for God.

Pray generationally. Mother generationally. Remember that your influence as a mother is not only for today, but will affect future generations. This takes us to a new level of mothering. Make every decision in the light of future generations, not just how it will affect you today.

You are a generation builder. *Nancy*

Look for the End Result

We all face trials, but the end result of trials makes them all worthwhile! James 1:2-4 NIV says, *"Consider it pure joy my brothers whenever you face trials of many kinds because you know that the testing of your faith develops perseverance. Perseverance must finish its work so that you may be MATURE AND COMPLETE, NOT LACKING ANYTHING!"* Now isn't that amazing? *Michelle*

- August 7 -

Can You Believe it?

Jeremiah lamented in Lamentations 4:12, *"The kings of the earth, and all the inhabitants of the world, would not have believed that the adversary and enemy should have entered into the gates of Jerusalem."* This was hard for the Jews to comprehend. However, we face a similar scenario today.

The enemy has entered the very sanctuary of the church with his life-destroying plans. Who is it that teaches young couples who are preparing for marriage? Pastors and church counselors. And what do many of them advise these young couples? To wait a few years before having children. To limit their family to one or two children and to use various methods of birth control.

Does this advice come from God's Word? No, it comes from the adversary who has broken into the very heart of the church. Can you comprehend it? *Nancy*

A Second Mother

Motherhood is more than children born of your own womb. Motherhood comes in many forms—adoption, fostering, and the often forgotten mentoring! How often do we hear the expression, "She is like a second mother to me"? Who are you mothering today? Opportunities abound to nurture and breathe love into many lives around you. *Michelle*

- August 8 -

Teaching Trust

David confessed in Psalm 22:9-10 NASB, *"You are He who brought me forth from the womb; You made me trust when upon my mother's breasts. Upon You I was cast from birth; You have been my God from my mother's womb."*

Dear mother, nursing your baby is not insignificant. You are preparing your baby for a relationship with God the Father. You are doing something even greater than feeding your baby as you put your baby to the breast. As your baby comes freely to you for comfort, food, and sustenance, you not only satisfy your baby, but you are teaching your baby how to trust in God.

What a beautiful and powerful assignment. *Nancy*

Dripping with Praise

Sometimes it's too easy to find fault in others, isn't it? Instead, I am going to look at all that is praiseworthy in my husband, my sons, my daughters, and my friends. In fact, I won't stop there, but I'll also extend into my community. May my lips drip with praise! May yours, too! *Michelle*

- August 9 -

Secret for Greatness

What is the criterion for greatness? Psalm 18:35 says, *"Thy gentleness hath made me great."* Society brainwashes us to think that we have to be well known or famous to be great. That's not what God says. He says that the anointing of gentleness will make you great. The mother who gently nurses her baby, cares for her little ones, and nurtures her family is not unimportant. Her gentle mothering reveals to the world God's compassionate and nurturing heart. In her gentle mothering, she wields a mighty force against the enemy as she trains children to love and serve God.

Don't despise gentleness, dear mother. Embrace it. Walk in a gentle spirit in your marriage and motherhood. It is not weakness. It is your anointing of greatness. *Nancy*

The Lowly Server

At times, we long for some "greatness." The disciples asked which of them would be the greatest. We know the answer. The lowly server is the greatest. This is comforting for us mothers. We are great through our lowly service. Imagine that? You imitate Christ through your service in your home. *Michelle*

Do You Fear a Fear?

Psalm 53:5 says, *"There they were in great fear, where no fear was."* The margin of my Bible says, *"They feared a fear."* One of Satan's greatest tactics is to bind us up with fear even when there is no valid reason for the fear. These deceptive fears immobilize you from fulfilling God's plan for your life. They debilitate you. Society fills women with deceptive fears.

"It would be dangerous to have a baby in my forties!" I beg your pardon. You are in your childbearing years until you reach menopause. "I may have a Down syndrome baby." And you may not, so what are you fearing? And if you did (which can happen to a mother of any age), this child would be your greatest blessing. "I've had two C-sections and my doctor says I can't have any more." There are many mothers who have seven and eight C-sections, and their womb is still as great as ever.

The "fears of a fear" keep coming. Will you give in to them or trust in God? *Nancy*

Enrich Others

I was sharing with my husband that there is no neutral path. We are either adding to or taking away from someone's experience. May our presence add positively and enrich those with whom we come in contact. I want my presence to add to everyone's day, not take away from it, don't you? *Michelle*

- August 11 -

Never Give In

Proverbs 14:1 says, *"Every wise woman buildeth her house: but the foolish plucketh it down with her hands."* Remember, mother, you are in the greatest building program in the nation. Men spend much time, effort, and finance to build great buildings that will all one day decay. You are building into eternal souls who will live forever.

You are also building strong, godly families who will impact this nation for God. I know that you may sometimes feel depressed, discouraged, or demoralized. But never give in! That's just the devil trying to stop you in your great building program. Keep on building. Keep on keeping on. Keep on praying. Keep on believing. God is with you. *Nancy*

Positive Changes

In my workout today, the trainer said, "You have to be uncomfortable for change to happen." Isn't that the truth? If I don't work hard enough to feel it, there will be no progress.

It is the same with our faith life. We often have to go through some discomfort in order for our faith to grow. Are you uncomfortable with some things in your life right now? Positive changes are on the horizon. Keep up the good fight. *Michelle*

I Am Doing a Great Work!

When Nehemiah came back from Babylon to build up the wall of Jerusalem, he encountered many adversaries. They were determined to stop his building project. They wanted to thwart God's purposes. On one occasion, they tried to get him to come down from the wall and meet them in the *"plain of Ono."*

But Nehemiah did not come down. He did not stop building! He sent a message saying, *"I AM DOING A GREAT WORK, so that I cannot come down: why should the work cease, whilst I leave it, and come down to you?"* (Nehemiah 6:3).

Mother, you are doing a great work. When your adversaries try to stop you, don't be tempted. Confess out loud, "I AM DOING A GREAT WORK, SO THAT I CANNOT COME DOWN." Don't come down from your high calling. That's the whole purpose of the enemy—to stop you from building a strong marriage and family. Don't you let him. *Nancy*

Parenting Like God

I love how God reveals Himself as our Father through the utter dependence of a child on a parent. My baby looks to me for everything—safety, protection, nourishment, love, encouragement, comfort, cleansing, understanding, security, and more. It is an amazing analogy of how we truly need God and how we must rely on Him for all things. The best part is, unlike me, He never fails His children! *Michelle*

- August 13 -

Promise of Great Things to Come!

Weddings are the blessing of God. He loves to draw a couple together and establish another godly family. When God's blessing is on the nation, there will be lots of weddings.

We will hear *"the voice of joy, and the voice of gladness, the voice of the bridegroom, and the voice of the bride, the voice of them that shall say, Praise the Lord of hosts; for the Lord is good; and His mercy endureth forever."* (Jeremiah 33:10-11).

Did you notice that there will be joy and gladness? A wedding should be a time of joyful celebration. It is not an inconsequential function, but the promise of great things to come—establishing another godly home, more babies, and all the blessings, ministries, visions, and godly dynasties that will come from these babies.

The opposite is true when God's judgment is on the nation. Joy, gladness, and weddings will cease (Jeremiah 7:34; 16:9; 25:10). *Nancy*

Beautify Your Home

Do you want to be more beautiful? Or would you like to have a more beautiful home? Psalm 147:1 NKJV says, *"Praise the LORD! For it is good to sing praises to our God; for it is pleasant and praise is beautiful."* Fill your home and your lips with praise. It will beautify both you and your home. You will also feel pleasant because the psalm says praise is pleasant. Praise the day away. *Michelle*

- August 13 -

The Best Life

Embrace your mothering career with all your heart. Love it. Be there and enjoy it rather than dreaming of some other life. You are living the best life. You have the most powerful career. You are training children who will determine the destiny of the nation and the course of history. You couldn't be doing anything more powerful or life-changing!

We were created to be nurturers. As we embrace the career of motherhood and acknowledge that this is God's perfect will for our lives, we enter into the joy and anointing of motherhood. Many mothers are frustrated because, although they love their children, they have not fully embraced their divine calling which God has given to them. Instead of complaining, enjoy to the full your mothering days. *Nancy*

Why Not Today?

I realized afresh how guilty I can be of taking some things for granted. I often take my health and my loved ones for granted, as though they will always be there for me.

This line of thinking made me want to doll-up a bit for my husband today! Before we were married, I always looked my best for him! Why not now?

My goal for today is to show my appreciation to my loved ones in tangible ways. *Michelle*

- August 14 -

A Tranquil Heart

Proverbs 14:30 NASB says, *"A tranquil heart is life to the body."* The word "tranquil" in the Hebrew means "curative, medicine, healing." A tranquil heart is medicine to your soul and healing to your body.

Maybe you are not feeling very tranquil at the moment! Everything is on top of you. Or, perhaps you are worrying over a certain situation in your life or family. How can you get a tranquil heart?

Put your trust in the Lord. Take your eyes off all you have to do and the things that worry you, and turn your eyes to the Lord. God is bigger than all your circumstances. Look to Him, and He will fill your heart with peace and tranquility. It is our attitude that determines the state of our heart. Put away all anger, bitterness, unforgiveness, tension and worry. They are negative to your body. Ask the Holy Spirit to cleanse you, wash over you, and fill your heart with His peace. You will even have new energy in your body. *Nancy*

Reveal God's Glory

"The glory of the Lord shall be revealed, and all flesh shall see it together" (Isaiah 40:5). This is true through Jesus Christ, and it is also true through you! What an honor to reveal the glory of the Lord to those around us. Keep up the amazing testimony of God's glory in your life. *Michelle*

- August 15 -

Spread the Truth

I want to be a Truth Spreader, don't you? Proverbs 15:7 NASB says, *"The lips of the wise spread knowledge."* We are constantly inundated with humanistic brainwashing. I am tired of it. It is time we promoted truth to our children and to everyone we meet wherever we go.

Be a TRUTH SPREADER today, and never be intimidated by your adversaries! But, of course, you'll have to seek after truth and know the truth before you can spread the truth. *Nancy*

A Child's Attitude

We learn so much from children. Their hearts are soft. They freely love, give, and forgive. They are resilient and do not hold onto bitterness. They are unselfish with their time and assets. Their faith is pure and strong. They smile, laugh, and dance frequently.

If we would learn to emulate these childish qualities while being responsible adults, what a world it would be! Jesus said, "Except ye be converted, and become as little children, ye shall not enter into the kingdom of heaven" (Matthew 18:3). *Michelle*

- August 16 -

Keep Praying

David cried out, *"For my love they are my adversaries: but I give myself unto prayer. And they have rewarded me evil for good, and hatred for my love"* (Psalm 109:4-5). David didn't deserve their hatred, and he could have reacted back with bitterness and anger.

Instead, he prayed! He didn't pray once, but gave himself to prayer. The words, "give myself unto" are in italics in the KJV, which means they have only been put in to make sense. It should read *"I am prayer."*

When people speak against you and hurt you, instead of reacting negatively, pray for them and bless them. To get the victory, you'll find you have to keep praying. You will have to become like David who confessed, *"I am prayer!" Nancy*

"You're Beautiful!"

Today my son said, "Mom, I think I will take your picture." I asked him if he could wait until I looked more presentable.

He answered, "Mom, you always look good, and I'm not kidding."

What a gift to always be beautiful in their eyes, even as we crawl out of bed! The home is truly where we get nourished. *Michelle*

- August 17 -

Health Secret

What kind of a face did you wake up with this morning? Gloomy and frowning? Or, sunny and happy?

Proverbs 17:22 GNB says, *"Being cheerful keeps you healthy. It is slow death to be gloomy all the time."* You can choose! Your spirit should rule your flesh.

Even if you feel miserable, put on a smile! Your heart will change to cheerful, and your children will start smiling, too! *Nancy*

Good Investment

If you don't take care of yourself, you will have little to nothing to offer your loved ones. Make sure you take care of yourself, so the rest of the family will be blessed.

Take the time to pray, eat right, exercise, and relax/rejuvenate so that you can have more to offer those around you. It is a good investment with great returns! *Michelle*

- August 18 -

Spirit, Soul, and Body

Are your children looking rosy and healthy? I am sure they are. You take great care to prepare three nutritious meals each day to make sure they will grow and become strong.

But your children are more than flesh and blood. They are body, soul, and spirit. Do you take as much time to prepare and nourish them spiritually as you do physically? We need to dish out to them daily meals of God's Word in order for them to grow strong in the spirit.

As I raised our children, my prayer and goal was I Thessalonians 5:23, *"The very God of peace sanctify you wholly; and I pray God your whole spirit and soul and body be preserved blameless unto the coming of our Lord Jesus Christ."*

Will their spirits be as well-nourished as their bodies when Jesus comes? *Nancy*

No Greater Privilege

"Life affords no greater responsibility, no greater privilege, than the raising of the next generation" (C. Everet Koop, M.D). So true! I am thankful for this privilege! *Michelle*

Top of the List

Do you write lists each day? I do. I would never remember all I have to do unless I wrote lists. Although, I have to confess, I rarely get through everything on my list!

The other morning I read Proverbs 4:7 in the Message Bible. It says, *"Above all and before all, do this: Get wisdom! Write this at the TOP OF YOUR LIST. Get understanding."* I thought that was a good idea.

Today I wrote at the top of my list: 1) Get Wisdom and Understanding. Then I realized that I can't get wisdom without delving into God's Word, which is my source of wisdom.

Immediately, I was inspired to do the most important thing of the day—read God's precious Word. *Nancy*

Try Mercy and Peace

I woke up curious as to how often the Bible mentions joy. When I looked it up, I noticed that joy was listed 205 times, mercy 363 times, and peace 451 times! I was surprised to learn that showing mercy and keeping peace were listed more than joy.

Today, I am going to work on showing mercy and keeping peace in my home and relationships, and see if joy follows. It likely will. *Michelle*

- August 20 -

Spirit Outpouring

Who does God pour out His Holy Spirit upon? Does He pour it out upon our TVs, cars, and material possessions? No, He pours out His Spirit upon our children.

Isaiah 44:3 says, *"I will pour out My Spirit on your offspring and My blessing on your descendants; and they will spring up among the grass like poplars by streams of water."*

Acts 2:17-18 says, *"I will pour out of My Spirit upon all flesh; and your sons and your daughters shall prophesy, and your young men shall see visions... and on My handmaidens I will pour out in those days of My Spirit; and they shall prophesy."*

The more children in our home, the more opportunity we have for the outpouring of the Holy Spirit. What a blessing. *Nancy*

Ten Percent More

Personal trainers often ask, "Can you give 10 percent more?" I asked myself, today, if I could smile 10 percent more. I hope you have a "smiley" day, too. Give that beautiful smile of yours 10 percent more action. I know I need the reminder. *Michelle*

More Valuable

Said the robin to the sparrow:
"I should really like to know
Why these anxious human beings
Rush about and worry so?"

Said the sparrow to the robin:
"Friend, I think that it must be
That they have no heavenly Father
Such as cares for you and me."

Jesus said that even a sparrow does not fall to the ground without our heavenly Father knowing. Then, He reminds us, *"Fear ye not therefore, ye are of more value than many sparrows"* (Matthew 10:29-31). There is nothing happening to you, even in the midst of your kitchen right now that He does know about. He has not forgotten you. He is with you to enable you right now. *Nancy*

Blessing of Family

What a blessing to be placed in a family, not only to serve and love them, but also to have the support of people that love you and are willing to help when you need a lift up. Praise God for the privilege of being in a family. *Michelle*

You Are What You Eat

They say you become what you eat. When you eat junk food, you'll deteriorate; hopefully, if you eat life-giving healthy food, you'll be healthy.

This applies spiritually, too. God's Word is life-giving. When we eat it, we grow mature and become more like Christ who is revealed in the Scriptures. Sadly, many are very skinny spiritually. If we only ate one physical meal a week, we would look anorexic! Yet, many rely solely on hearing a sermon at church once a week for their spiritual nourishment. It's not enough to grow spiritually strong and healthy. We need to feed daily.

As my husband says, "We must feast on the truth until the truth becomes us." *Nancy*

God Makes No Mistakes

The best part about our awesome responsibility as parents is knowing that God ordains every conception. When He visits us and gives us a child to raise for Him, He knows exactly into whose hands He places that eternal soul.

He makes no mistakes!

He trusts us to fulfill that responsibility well. He is confident in our abilities, realizing that we are but dust, but HE is our Strength and our Helper! *Michelle*

- August 24 -

Don't Get Offended

Have you been in discord with people? What's the situation now? Are you estranged from someone with whom you had a dispute, or are you still in good fellowship? Disagreement should not spoil our fellowship. That is very small-minded. God's love and forgiveness in us is bigger than any quarrel (Colossians 3:12-15).

In Acts 15:1-6, we read that the apostles had *"great dissension and debate"* together, but they didn't get offended. After the dissension, they were still in fellowship with one another.

This is our victory in Christ, in the home, and with others outside the home—to stay in fellowship even when we disagree. *Nancy*

What Are You Speaking?

Today is a wonderful day to speak words of praise to the members of your household. This is how we build up our homes, isn't it?

Today, I plan to verbalize as much praise and thankfulness as possible to my husband and children. This should help me keep a positive focus as well. *Michelle*

- August 25 -

Upset the World

Are you causing any trouble to the world around you?

"Oh no," you reply. "I seek to make everyone happy."

Sorry, wrong answer. That's not the testimony of the early believers. In Acts 16:20 the people of Thyatira said that Paul and Silas *"do exceedingly trouble our city."* When they got to Thessalonica, the people cried out, *"These that have turned the world upside down are come higher also... and these all do contrary to the decrees of Caesar"* (Acts 17:6-7). The NASB translates it as *"men who have upset the world."*

We are not in this world to assimilate to the world, but to upset the world—to challenge their deceptions, expose the darkness, and oppose their evil ways. We are not here to be popular, but to disturb the status quo.

Am I upsetting the enemy's kingdom? Are you? *Nancy*

Impacting Culture

As mothers, we are impacting our culture, our future, and the future beyond us! How? In our relationships with our own children and those with whom we have contact. May the impression you leave with them strengthen and equip them in every way to be fit soldiers in Christ's army. Leave a godly heritage. *Michelle*

- August 26 -

Can You Stop God's Faithfulness?

Why am I so lacking in faith when I have experienced the faithfulness of God over and over again? I often have to ask myself this question, but there is one fact that I cannot deny—my unbelief does not affect God's faithfulness.

Romans 3:3-4 NASB say, *"What then? If some did not believe, their unbelief will not nullify the faithfulness of God, will it? May it never be! Rather, let God be found true, though every man be found a liar."* I love J. B. Phillip's translation, which says, *"Can you imagine that their faithlessness could disturb the faithfulness of God? Of course not!"*

You may be saying, "I don't know where money is coming for our food next week. How could we trust God for another baby?" Even though you find it hard to believe God, it won't change His faithfulness to provide. He waits for you to take a step of faith. To read more on this topic, check out this link: http://bit.ly/IsGodAble). *Nancy*

Pride and Joy

The pride and joy you take in your children is only a glimmer of the pride and joy that the Father takes in you. You are loved beyond comprehension! When we grasp this truth and believe it, we are able to have our tanks filled and can pour out tons of love around us. *Michelle*

Open Your Doors

Gaius had a generous hospitable heart. He was a host to Paul and to *"the whole church"* (Romans 16:23).

Are the doors of your home open to hospitality? This ministry is not an option. It is the lifestyle of the kingdom of God. It is an extension of your mothering and homemaking anointing. It is one of the "good works" God intends for women (I Timothy 5:10). It is a biblical doctrine that starts in Genesis and weaves through pages of the Bible until the last book of Revelation.

If you are not used to flowing in this ministry, start in a little way. Ask one person to join your meal table. Soon you will want to invite more and more people into your home. *Nancy*

Trials Before Patience

Remember this hymn?

> *Must Jesus bear the cross alone, And all the world go free?*
> *No, there's a cross for everyone, And there's a cross for me.*

Romans 5:3-4 reminds us that patience comes from tribulation. If you are facing trials today, focus on the fruit that will be born in your character as a result. One of my favorite sayings is, "There is an upside to every downside!" *Michelle*

Our Incomprehensible God

We will never comprehend the fullness of God, and all His attributes, even though we search after Him all our lives. Yet, this should be our greatest study, not only for us, but for our children. Everything else is insignificant compared to the knowledge of God. Raise your children to always be in awe of our incomprehensible God. Never allow your children to take God for granted.

The wonderful thing is that we will learn more and more of Him in the eternal realm. Even there, we will not know God fully because we will not be infinite, but we will continually understand more and more insights of His majesty which will keep us worshipping all eternity (Revelation 4:8-11).

John Dick writes, "It will never reach a limit beyond which there is nothing to be discovered, and when ages after ages have passed away, He will still be the incomprehensible God." *Nancy*

Worry Waste

Do not bother wasting one second of this precious day in worry. We cannot even make one hair black or white (Matthew 5:36). This should give us great peace. After all, we are children of our perfect Father. I am so glad that He is in control, and not me. He will never disappoint. Have an amazing day! *Michelle*

Cheerfully Please God

What is your goal? Paul confessed, *"We make it our aim, whether present or absent to be well pleasing to Him"* (II Corinthians 5:9 NKJV). Is our attitude in our home acceptable to God? Do we go about our household tasks, even the humdrum, cheerfully pleasing God?

Are the words we speak to our husband and children well pleasing to Him? David's prayer in Psalm 19:14 is a good prayer to pray each morning, *"Let the words of my mouth, and the meditation of my heart, be acceptable in Thy sight, O Lord, my strength, and my redeemer."*

What is our daily lifestyle teaching our children? *Nancy*

Don't Neglect Couple Time

It is so important to have "couple time" in a marriage, isn't it? I know that this can be difficult at times. I have the privilege of organizing my whole day around the fact that tonight I have a date with my husband.

Making "couple time" in your marriage is so good for both of you. Don't neglect special time for the two of you. Too much rests upon your relationship. A strong marriage is a godly testimony. *Michelle*

- August 30 -

A Chain Reaction

God continually wants to encourage and cheer us up. But, how does He do it? He looks for one of His servants, one who listens to His voice, to go to the disheartened and strengthen them.

Paul sent Timothy to the Thessalonian believers to *"strengthen and encourage"* their faith (1 Thessalonians 3:2 NASB). He then told them to encourage others, especially the fainthearted (I Thessalonians 5:15 NASB).

One believer cheers up someone who is discouraged, and then that person cheers up someone else. Are you part of the chain reaction? *Nancy*

The Power of Thankfulness

Thankfulness is a very powerful thing. In the harder moments of life, stop a second and offer a prayer of thankfulness. Watch, and be amazed at the results.

During the delivery of a baby, I often stop and pray, "Lord, thank you for my womb, for the new life within it, and for my body operating as it should." It is incredible how much better the contractions feel!

Gratitude is your secret weapon! *Michelle*

- August 31 -

Full-Proof Answer

Are you feeling down in the dumps? Are you depressed and dejected? I've got the answer. The foolproof way to get out of your despondency is to bless someone else.

Think of someone else who is in need. Is there a young mother who is overwhelmed and needs help? Invite her and the children to have lunch with you or bring a meal to them. Do you know a mother who is sick? Make her a pot of soup and homemade bread and take it to her. You'll soon forget your own problems. You'll be wondering what they were!

Mark Twain said, "The best way you can cheer yourself up is to cheer someone else up." *Nancy*

Greater is He

God promises us in Isaiah 41:10 RSV, *"Fear not, for I am with you, be not dismayed, for I am your God; I will strengthen you, I will help you, I will uphold you with My victorious right hand."*

Not only does God strengthen and help us, but He upholds us! Not only does He uphold us, but upholds us with His VICTORIOUS right hand! What else do you need?

Remember, too, that *"**Greater is He** that is in you, than he that is in the world"* (I John 4:4). Let's not lose sight of God's promises, *Michelle*

- September 1 -

Learning to Fight

We would rather not be in a battle, would we? And yet, it is unavoidable. We can't get out of it. We are in an ongoing battle between the kingdom of God and the kingdom of darkness. Because we are engaged in this battle, we have to learn how to fight.

Paul said in II Corinthians 6:4-10, *"In all things approving ourselves... by the word of truth, by the power of God, by the armor of righteousness on the right hand and on the left."* We have to learn to fight with both hands, on the offensive and the defensive, and guarding on all sides. We must hold the shield of faith with one hand and wield the sword of the Spirit (the Word of God) with the other.

Teach your children how to fight with both hands. Raise children who will stand in the fight instead of being knocked down by the enemy. *Nancy*

Be Strong

Are you feeling overwhelmed with the daunting tasks you face today? Remember how daunting the task was to rebuild the temple that was lying in complete ruin? And, what did God say? *"**Be strong**, all ye people of the land, saith the Lord, and work: for I am with you"* (Haggai 2:4).

He is with us in our work, and we will not fail since He calls us to do it. *Michelle*

- September 2 -

Flesh and Blood

I am sure you have memorized and believe John 8:32, *"Ye shall know the truth, and the truth shall make you free."*

We quote this Scripture glibly, but do we really know what we are saying? It is only the truth that you **know** that will set you free. When you get an understanding and revelation of the truth, and embrace it with your whole heart, it will free you. It is the truth, which becomes "flesh and blood," that revolutionizes your life.

Feed from the Word, and feed it to your family. Receive it into your life, apply it faithfully, and impart it to your children. *Nancy*

Reject Self-Absorption

Today, I am wearing my "I love my husband" wristband. It is an excellent way for me to keep God's command at the forefront of my mind. To love one another brings such blessings; yet, we are often prone to being self-absorbed, rather than others-centered.

Create a day of overflowing love and joy in your marriage and home. *Michelle*

- September 3 -

A Future and a Hope

Can I guess that Jeremiah 29:11 is one of your favorite Scriptures? *"For I know the thoughts that I think toward you, saith the Lord, thoughts of peace, and not of evil, to give you an expected end."* Most translations render it, *"to give you a future and a hope."* Truly our God is a God of hope and has our future marked out for us.

But have you been a little naughty and claimed this Scripture without reading it in context? A message from the Lord of hosts precedes the promise! "This is what I want you to do first," God says: "1) Build houses, 2) Plant gardens, 3) Bear children, 4) Encourage your children to have children, 5) Increase your family and don't diminish, 6) Pray for your city, and 7) Don't be deceived by the prophets in the midst of you."

Now, you can claim your favorite promise. *Nancy*

Keep On Despite Trials

I believe having a great attitude in the face of trying circumstances is an excellent way to emulate Christ. It was also taught to us by the apostle Paul, who managed to fulfill his mission despite countless trials and even imprisonment.

Of course, it doesn't come naturally. We will need plenty of help from above. Thankfully, that help is only a prayer away. *Michelle*

- September 4 -

Jesus Is My Lord

When we confess with our mouth that Jesus Christ is Lord and Savior of our lives, we are born again (Romans 10:9-10). We first meet Him as Savior, but as we walk with Him we get to know Him in many other ways.

We get to know Him as Altogether lovely, Bread of life, Chiefest among ten thousand, Door of the sheep, Emmanuel, Forgiver of my sins, Gracious, Hope of the needy, Intercessor, Justifier, Keeper of my soul, Lamb of God, Merciful High Priest, Nourisher, Overcomer, Prince of Peace, Quieter of my soul, Redeemer, Sanctifier, Tried and True, Upholder of all things, Valiant Warrior, Wonderful Savior, eXalted, Yesterday, today and forever, and Zion's Eternal King.

In Him are hid all the treasures of wisdom and knowledge. All our thoughts and meditations of Him will never be enough to fathom all of who He is as God and Savior. *Nancy*

What's Your Affirmation?

My challenging affirmation for today is, "My circumstances will not define my attitude!"

All too often I get caught up in a frustrating moment, and my attitude turns sour. Today, I am going to practice having a contagiously wonderful attitude, even when I face parenting and homeschooling challenges.

I am FREE to have a fantastic attitude! *Michelle*

- September 5 -

The Center of Attention

I often hear the remark from young mothers that they wouldn't want to have too many children, because they couldn't give each one quality time. If only they could see the wonder of being a baby in a large family! I watch my two-year-old granddaughter, the eighth child in her family, being the queen of the domain. She is not only adored by her parents, but doted on from morning until night by her older sisters and brothers.

Her older sisters play with her all day, dressing her up in all kinds of clothes. She's a "real live baby doll!" Wherever she goes, they go! Whatever she does, they laugh! Whatever facial expression she makes, they say, "Isn't she so cute?"

What firstborn, or even second or third-born, could receive this constant attention? Even mother has more time to give attention to her baby because the older children are able to help in the home. It's the babies in bigger families that receive the most attention. *Nancy*

He Chose Me

Anytime I struggle with self-doubt or a feeling of being overwhelmed, I recall that God chose me, and He makes no mistakes! Obviously, I am able to complete the task, because He put me here. I can "parent" and "wife" sufficiently.

It is the same for you. We are more than able, and we are in the right place at the right time. God has ordained it. *Michelle*

- September 6 -

God Loves Babies

Acts 7:20 Amplified tells us that when Moses was born he was *"BEAUTIFUL in the sight of God."* I also think of II Samuel 12:24 which tells us that when Solomon was born, *"the Lord LOVED him."* These incredible Scriptures reveal the heart of God towards children.

God loves all babies. I picture Him looking down with love, oohing and aahing over each new baby He creates. He looks upon the innocent babe and sees all the beauty of His creation, all the gifts and talents He has put in this child, and the destiny that awaits him. Each child is ultimately HIS child, but He releases the babe with a clean slate into the hands of parents.

How seriously we should receive this charge. We have a fulltime career, and our employer is the King of kings and Lord of lords. *Nancy*

It's in Your Power

Did you know that you wield a mighty power? You have the power to create the atmosphere of your home. You can make it a place where people gravitate in order to be built up, empowered, and refueled. Isn't that amazing? I want my home to be like this, don't you? *Michelle*

- September 7 -

We Taste with Our Eyes

"We taste with our eyes as well as our palate." Isn't this true?

It's not enough to cook a nourishing meal; we must prepare the table to receive the meal. When a table is laid with a tablecloth and set beautifully, with a candle or "a touch of love" to make it look inviting, the food tastes even better.

"But, how do I do this when I have little ones?" you ask. You don't have to do it all. Teach your children how to set the table nicely and creatively. You will be amazed at what they can do. As your children have turns, they will become quite competitive as to who can set it the most attractively and invitingly.

Proverbs 9:1-2 NASB says, *"Wisdom has built her house... she has prepared her food, she has mixed her wine; she has also SET HER TABLE."* It is a wise woman who sets her table, for she knows the blessings that will come from it. *Nancy*

Set the Trend

People tend to be followers. Behaviors and attitudes are catchy. If we want our culture to have a different view of family, women, children, or even hospitality, we need to exemplify it so others will want it, too.

All we need to do is ENJOY our lives and our roles. It is a win-win proposition—for us and for those watching. Never underestimate your impact in the world outside your walls. *Michelle*

- September 8 -

What Do You Want?

- I want children (and grandchildren) who are growing into the likeness of Christ!
- I want children who love righteousness and hate evil!
- I want children who know truth and stand for truth!
- I want children who will not compromise, or be tainted, with the spirit of this world!
- I want children who will not give into the lust of the flesh, the lust of the eyes, and the pride of life, but who rejoice do the will of God!
- I want children who love the Word of God and love to pray!
- I want children who love to be with the people of God!
- I want children who will pursue God and blaze across this world with the Gospel and the message of truth!

Is this your prayer, too? *Nancy*

I want to Be a Blessing

My motivational thought for today is this: in order to bless someone with my presence, my presence had better be a blessing! My goal is to bless those in my presence, and by God's grace, I will be a blessing. *Michelle*

- September 9 -

Teach Your Children to Work

When our grandson, Arden, first got his horses, his parents told him it would be his responsibility to work to provide for the hay and all expenses. He began to call up neighbors. Serene overheard one conversation...

"Good morning. This is Arden Allison. I am Nancy Campbell's grandson. I am 12 years old, but I can work like a man!"

What a great confession. It didn't take long for him to get work, and he has been paying for hay and expenses for over a year now.

Are we training our sons to be providers or to rely on their parents or the government like so many do today? They need to get into the habit of working hard while they are young. It is a grief to me to see lazy young men who don't know how to "get stuck in." At 70-plus years, I can work harder than they can. They will not be marriageable material!

Let's raise real men. *Nancy*

Relax and Rejuvenate

Do you feel overwhelmed with so many things to do and constant demands on your time? I like to remember that Jesus was in that position, too. What did He do? He retreated to a quiet place every now and then to pray and rejuvenate. Sometimes I retreat for a quick soak in the tub and some quiet time with God, and then I'm ready to begin again. Have a rejuvenating prayer-filled day! *Michelle*

- September 10 -

Now and Forever

Here's a promise to pray and believe for your children, *"My Spirit which is upon you, and My words which I have put in your mouth shall not depart from your mouth, nor from the mouth of your offspring, nor from the mouth of your offspring's offspring, says the Lord, from **now** and forever"* (Isaiah 59:21 NASB).

We must make sure that we are walking in the power of the Holy Spirit and filling our lives with God's Words so that we can faithfully pass them on to our children. They must become so ingrained in their hearts that they will naturally pass them on to their children and all future generations forever. *Nancy*

Key to Contentment

When we focus on how we can be better molded into the image of Christ by the Spirit of God, and less on how we feel those around us need molding, we find contentment. Our joy is often robbed by dwelling on perceived deficits in others. Our time would be better and more profitably spent working on our own deficits.

Luke 6:42 says, *"Cast out first the beam out of thine own eye, and then thou shalt see clearly to pull out the mote that is in thy brother's eye."*

In marriage, it is not so much about finding the right person, as it is about becoming the right person for your spouse. *Michelle*

A Pure Spring

It is a delight to behold the reflection of God's creation in a pure spring, isn't it? You can't see anything in a muddied spring. Proverbs 25:26 ESV says, *"Like a muddied spring and a polluted fountain is a righteous man who gives way to the wicked."* May God save us from becoming murky and muddy, which is what happens when we compromise with evil.

Notice this Scripture is not talking about unbelievers, but about believers who give way to the wicked! It's a sad state of affairs when the righteous lose their testimony. Let's be on the offensive and stand up for truth and righteousness—in our homes and in the nation.

And remember, when we become muddied, people cannot see a clear and accurate reflection of Jesus in us. *Nancy*

Change Focus

Are you enjoying all that today has to offer? Sometimes it means rising above your current circumstances and changing focus. It takes effort, but again, is always worth it. Enjoy your day. There will never be another exactly like it. *Michelle*

- September 12 -

Never Give Up

"Blessed is the man who PERSEVERES under trial" (James 1:12 NASB). The Greek word for "perseveres" is *hupomeno*, which means "to endure or sustain a load of miseries, adversities, persecutions or provocations in faith and patience."

Are you going through a trial? Don't give up, dear mother. Keep enduring. Keep trusting God. He will not leave you in your hour of difficulty. You may not be delivered from it immediately, but you will be sustained through it as you place your trust in Him. *Nancy*

More Than Feeding

The Scriptures refer to nursing, not only as a source of physical nourishment, but emotional comfort.

Psalm 22:9 NIV says, *"You brought me out of the womb. You made me* **trust** *at my mother's breasts."* And Isaiah 66:11 NIV says, *"For you will nurse and be* **satisfied** *at her* **comforting** *breasts; you will drink deeply and* **delight** *in her overflowing abundance."*

When you nurse your baby, you do so much more than simply feed! You teach trust. You satisfy, comfort, and give delight to you baby. You are powerfully privileged, not tied down or inconvenienced. *Michelle*

- September 13 -

Expose the Darkness

God encourages us to take heed to the sure prophecy that He has given us in His Word. He says it is a *"light that shineth in a dark place"* (II Peter 1:19). We cannot do without God's Word, for it exposes the dirt and darkness in this world.

The more we are filled with the light of His Word, the more we will discern darkness and deception. In fact, if the light of truth does not fill my mind and heart, I will be drawn into the darkness.

I am either becoming part of the darkness (often without realizing it), or I am a light exposing the darkness. Which are you? Which are you training your children to be? *Nancy*

Enjoy Your Husband

Think of every way possible you can enjoy your husband; and no matter what, you will find something to relish! Focus on the positive in your marriage, and you'll be so glad you did.

There are always things to appreciate if you take the time to contemplate them. *Michelle*

- September 14 -

Thank You SO MUCH!

Are you teaching your children to show appreciation? Not out of duty, but because they really are grateful? Are they in the habit of saying, "Thank you"?

I remember when we took our grandson, Crusoe, out to dinner for his 13ᵗʰ birthday. Continually throughout the evening, he exclaimed, "Thank you, Nana and Granddad, SO much." All the grandchildren are the same way. They are so appreciative of the tiniest thing that is done for them or given to them and are spontaneous in expressing their thanks and appreciation.

This kind of attitude is "caught" rather than "taught." Do your children see you appreciating others? Do they see you thanking your husband and showing real appreciation when he does some little thing for you? Do you say "Thank you" to your children when they do something for you? Encourage this habit to flow in your family. *Nancy*

Always Grateful

In life we have so much to relish and enjoy. All that we have is a precious gift—life, family, friends, nourishing food, and God's beauty in nature. A positive perspective and outlook make a huge difference in the moments that make up my day. I need to remember that it is all to be treasured as an amazing gift and should never be taken for granted. *Michelle*

- September 15 -

Consolidated

God wants you and your family to be settled and established in your convictions, not weakened or toppled because of persecution or difficulties. I Peter 5:10 says, *"The God of all grace...by Christ Jesus, after that ye have suffered a while, make you perfect, establish, strengthen, settle you."* The word "settle" is *themelioo* and means, "to lay a foundation, to consolidate."

Even when you go through a period of suffering, God will not forsake you. He will come, restore, and settle you. Let Him do His work in your life. *Nancy*

Christ in Me

I looked around the house today and wondered, "Is it ever good enough?" It seems that regardless of the time and effort exerted, the house is never quite in the order I would like it.

Then I realized that, like my house, I am not in perfect order either. Yet I have all that I need in Christ to be made perfect! In Him, I am perfectly in order in the Father's eyes.

Suddenly the state of the house seemed fine, and I had a huge smile on my face! *Michelle*

- September 16 -

First Things First

What was the first thing that God did after He created the man and woman? He blessed them (Genesis 1:28). How amazing to be *"blessed of the Lord which made heaven and earth"* (Psalm 115:15).

God loves to bless His people. It is inherit in Him to bless. Because we are created in His likeness, it should also be natural for us to bless, too. Ask God to make you a blesser as He is.

Bless your husband with loving and kind words. Bless your children with positive words from the time you wake in the morning until you go to bed at night. Bless them with your prayers. Bless everyone you meet. *Nancy*

Childlike Trust

Trusting the Lord for our salvation and our lives does not mean that life suddenly becomes smooth and perfect. Trusting the Lord with our finances does not mean we suddenly become wealthy. Trusting the Lord with fertility does not guarantee a large family. As in all areas of life, we simply trust Him for His will to be accomplished in our lives and that all things belong to Him. He blesses that childlike trust in Him. *Michelle*

- September 17 -

A Bereaved Nation

Did you know that a nation can be bereaved? Ezekiel 36:12-14 NASB says, *"Yes, I will cause men—My people Israel—to walk on you and possess you* (the mountains of Israel), *so that you will become their inheritance and never again bereave them of children."*

Is our nation bereaved of children? Yes. There are millions of children who have not been born because of abortion and contraception.

God-believing couples have refused to obey God's command to *"be fruitful and multiply"* and to bless the nation with godly seed. The nation is now bereaved of godliness, truth, and integrity. It is deprived of "salt" and "light."

Where are the righteous voters? Where is justice in the courts and the streets? The land is bereaved because of disobedience. *Nancy*

Kitchen Toys

Sometimes the best toys are right in the kitchen! I love how children can entertain themselves and bring us joy all at the same time! Today, my kitchen pots and pans were filled with creative and squirmy little bodies! The children used the lids as hats and had a jolly fun time. Have a fun-filled time at your house today! *Michelle*

- September 18 -

We Do It Together

*"As for us, **we** will walk in the name of the Lord our God forever and ever"* (Micah 4:5 NASB).

Is this your family testimony? It's not only you and your husband walking in God's ways, but *"we"*—you and your children. Together, we stand true to the Lord. Together, we gather each day to read God's Word and pray. Together, we resist evil and raise a voice for righteousness. Together, we go to church and fellowship with the saints each week.

We do not deviate. We do not slacken. We do not make excuses, or our family strength will weaken.

We make these commitments a habit in our lives so that not only our present generation, but our family generations to come will continue trusting in the name of the Lord. Will you say "Amen" with me? *Nancy*

With Gladness

"Make a joyful noise unto the Lord, all ye lands. Serve the Lord with gladness: come before His presence with singing" (Psalm 100:1-2).

Serve the Lord with **gladness** in your home today. It's another day the Lord has made for you. Fill your home with singing. It is a joy to be renewed and remade from the deadness of sin into the newness of life! *Michelle*

- September 19 -

Is Jesus Welcome in Your Life?

Jesus said, *"Whosoever shall receive this child in My name receiveth Me: and whosoever shall receive Me receiveth Him that sent Me"* (Luke 9:48). The word "receive" is *dechomai* and means "to receive deliberately what is offered."

It's not the attitude of, "Well, if God gives us another baby, we'll somehow survive!"

No, it is one of, "I'm anticipating another baby. I will welcome, with open arms, all the babies God gives me." It is not only receiving the blessing of a baby, but welcoming God into your life!

Isn't it amazing that God says that when we receive a baby, we actually receive Him? That changes our attitude, doesn't it? *Nancy*

We're on a Journey

Today was great, and tomorrow will be even better. Like you, I am on a journey of sanctification, and each day brings us closer to the finish line. Look how far we have come!

How invigorating and motivating to walk closer and closer with our Lord as we journey along serving Him. Each new day brings more and more potential. Praise God! *Michelle*

- September 20 -

A Full House

I read recently that the home is the emptiest place in America during the day. God never intended the home to be empty. Jesus told the parable of the man who made a big banquet and told his servant to *"Go out into the highways and hedges, and compel them to come in, that my house may be filled"* (Luke 14:23).

This is a picture of God's house. He wants His home to be filled. And, of course, because we are to be like Him, He wants our homes to be filled, too—not only filled with furniture and décor, but filled with people. He wants them to be filled with family togetherness—food, feasting, friendship, fellowship, and fun.

When a mother leaves her home and the family members scatter each day, the home is fragmented. The home is meant to be the strength of the nation where the family learns to work and grow stronger in God together. *Nancy*

Little by Little

Today, I held my tongue and responded with patience to a child instead. One small victory at a time! Little by little we grow, don't we? What is your victory today? *Michelle*

- September 21 -

Look Out, World!

Your home is a haven providing protection,
Filled with joy and peace and lots of affection,
It's God's chosen place for your husband and you,
To raise godly children, righteous and true,
You're making it a sanctuary from the evil around
So you can train children to be whole and sound,
The right time is coming when you'll send them out,
Empowered with God's Spirit—world, look out!

Nancy

No Defeat

Are you winning your battle today? It's not too late to turn the tide! The beauty of time is that each moment you can start over. No need to be defeated! *Michelle*

- September 22 -

The Yearning Womb

There is no stronger emotion than the yearning of a mother's heart. It is beautiful, and it is powerful. The source of this yearning (or we could say, "wombing") is in the heart of God.

We see a glimpse of God's heart and our own emotions in Jeremiah 31:20 NKJB where God yearns over His people, Israel, *"Is Ephraim My dear son?...Therefore My heart yearns for him. I will surely have mercy on him, declares the Lord."*

The word "yearns" is *meah,* which is Hebrew for womb, and the phrase "have mercy (or compassion) on him" is *racham,* another word for womb. This word is sometimes used to describe God's compassion and other times refers to the literal womb.

The womb is linked with compassion. As we embrace our womb, we flow in the anointing of compassion, and we reveal this powerful attribute of God to our children and to the world. *Nancy*

Treasure Them

Smile! As often as possible! More than normal! Love and adore the people in your life, and let them know how you treasure them. In return, you will have an amazing day. *Michelle*

- September 23 -

A Walking Picture

How humbling to think that every part of our womanly functions are born in the heart of God. He understands the emotions of pregnancy, birth, and nursing a baby. You do not experience these alone. God designed them, and He understands every feeling.

Isaiah 46:3-4 NASB says, *"The house of Israel, you who have been* **borne by Me from birth**, *and have been* **carried from the womb**... *even to your graying years* **I shall bear you**! *I have done it, and* **I shall carry you; and I shall bear you.**"

As you welcome the creating of another child in your womb, as well as giving birth and nurturing, you are a walking picture of God's heart and character. What a privilege! *Nancy*

Make It a Great Day

Embrace this day and all it has to offer. Pour love and sunshine into everyone's life that you touch today. Make it a great day. Your heavenly Father will give you all the strength you need to accomplish this. *Michelle*

- September 24 -

Embrace Your Womb

As women, our womb is our most distinguishing characteristic. A blatant fact is that there are only two kinds of people in this world: 1) a man without a womb—the man, and 2) a man with a womb—the woman.

It is our womb that makes us a woman. What a tragedy to despise who we are! Such is the deception of Satan!

You may like to read some different terms for your womb—seat of compassion, garden of life, safe haven of love, house of life, nesting place, palace of a child, sanctuary, cradle of the unborn, God's creative workshop, knitting place, holy place, and the secret place (Psalm 139:15).

Don't miss out on being who God created you to be. *Nancy*

Throw out Refined Foods

One of the best things you can do in order to be strong and fit as a mother is to eat right. Healthy eating gives your body the proper fuel to manage your daily tasks. This is a very worthwhile pursuit and will reap many benefits. *Michelle*

My Confession

"Christ in you, the hope of glory" (Colossians 1:27).

> *The greatest mystery in the entire universe,*
> *Greater than loads of money in my purse,*
> *Is that Christ, the Son of God, lives in me,*
> *Making His abode and setting me free!*

> *No longer living in defeat and despair*
> *Because joy and hope in Christ I share,*
> *Forgetting all worry and discontentment*
> *For in Christ I have mirth and merriment.*

> *Bursts of anger and hate no longer flow*
> *Because His longsuffering in me I know,*
> *Christ in me, the fullness of glory!*
> *This is my testimony and my story!*

Nancy

Try it!

I am going to stop and smile every single time before I open my mouth to speak to anyone. It is an experiment for me, but my theory is that the day will go better! Would you like to be part of my experiment?
Michelle

- September 26 -

A Surprising Truth

Do you know how Jesus referred to women? Here's a little surprise for you. In Matthew 19 we read how the Pharisees asked Him about divorce. Jesus answered in verse 4, *"Have ye not read, that He which made them in the beginning made them male and female?"*

The Greek word for "female" is *thelus* coming from the root word *thele,* which literally means, "the nipple of a woman's breast, to suckle, to nurse."

In other words, Jesus said that God originally made women to be suckling mothers. Now, that's a little different to what society tells you, isn't it? However, I think it is more important to listen to the One who created us than mere man, don't you? *Nancy*

Happily Serving

I am planning a surprise for my husband. I love how terrific it makes us feel when we are doing something for someone else. Serving is uplifting and exciting when done with the proper perspective. Nobody forces us to serve; we do it willingly. In return, we receive joy and many other benefits. Happily serve today. *Michelle*

- September 27 -

Godly or Heathen?

Jeremiah 10:25 says, *"Pour out Thy fury upon the heathen that know Thee not, and upon the families that call not on Thy name."*

On whom does God pour out His fury? The heathen. Anyone else? Yes, the families. What families? The families who do not call upon the name of the Lord. Ouch!

As a family, do you call upon the Lord together? Forgive me for saying it, but this Scripture tells us that if we don't call upon the Lord, we may as well be heathen.

Do you gather as a family to cry out to God for your city and nation? The Hebrew word "call" is *qara*. It does not mean to say a little quiet prayer, but "to cry out aloud, to roar, or to summon God's aid."

What will happen when God-fearing families put aside lesser activities and call upon the Lord together? *Nancy*

Keep on Trying

How did you do with smiling before speaking? I failed often, although I smiled much more than normal and noticed a huge difference. I am going to try it again today. It is going to take more practice for me! How about you? *Michelle*

- September 28 -

Which Life?

Are we living in the flesh or allowing the life of Jesus Christ to live through us? What is the character of Jesus? Here are seven aspects of the spirit of Jesus to line up with our lives.

The character of Jesus is the spirit of LOVE. (John 13:34-35; 15:13; Galatians 5:22).
The character of Jesus is the spirit of SERVING. (John 13:13-17; Philippians 2:7; Matthew 20:28)
The character of Jesus is the spirit of OBEDIENCE. (Matthew 26:36-42; Philippians 2:8; Hebrews 5:8).
The character of Jesus is the spirit of HUMILITY. (Matthew 11:29; Philippians 2:8; Colossians 3:12).
The character of Jesus is the spirit of FORGIVENESS. (Luke 23:34; Colossians 3:13).
The character of Jesus is the spirit of PATIENCE and LONGSUFFERING. (Galatians 5:22-23; Colossians 3:12-13).
The character of Jesus is the spirit of UNSELFISHNESS. (Philippians 2:4-8; I Peter 2:21-24).

Will your husband and children see the character of Jesus in you today? *Nancy*

Can He Wait to Come Home?

What can I do to adore my husband today? I want to build him up, along with my children and family. Husbands need attention and adoration as much as children. I will start by being sweet so that he can't wait to be home! *Michelle*

Restfully Busy

"My people... have forgotten their resting place" (Jeremiah 50:6). Do you sometimes forget that you have a resting place? Our 21st century lives are so frantically busy that often we live in a state of turmoil instead of a state of rest. But your Savior, Jesus Christ, wants you to live and abide in Him, which is a place of rest because He lives in rest.

Nothing takes Him by surprise. Nothing gets Him upset. He doesn't get into a stew and worry Himself sick. He is in control of all things and every detail of your life. In the midst of the whirlwind of life all around you, your soul can live in rest. The hymn says,

> *There is a place of quiet rest,*
> *Near to the heart of God,*
> *A place where sin cannot molest,*
> *Near to the heart of God.*

Why not live a restfully busy life instead of a frantically busy life? *Nancy*

Savor Each Moment

The moments in life pass ever so quickly, with or without our consent. We have little control over each day, so why not enjoy the ride? Let's savor every moment of the day as a gift from God! *Michelle*

- September 30 -

What's Your Choice?

Is the pace of life getting on top of you? Are you living on the edge? If so, it sounds like you are involved in too many things. God has an answer for you. The Knox translation of Hosea 11:11 says, *"And in their own home, says the Lord, I will give them rest."* When your home is out of order and you are living under pressure, it's time to come home. Cut back some of your activities. Say "No" to extra involvements.

"But all these things are important," you protest.

It's your choice—continue living in a state of stress, or do what God wants you to do, and start living life in your home! God gives the principles, but we have to obey them. Isaiah 30:15 says, *"In returning and rest shall ye be saved; in quietness and confidence shall be your strength."* But have you read the next three words? *"You would not!"*

What is your response? "Yes, Lord, I'll do it Your way," or "No thanks, I'll keep on my merry-go-round way of life." *Nancy*

Do You Need an Answer?

People laugh at me because I see children as the answer to so many issues. Struggling with pride? Raise a child! Feeling unloved or lonely? Raise a child! Feeling like you want to do more for God? Raise a child! Struggling with finding a real sense of purpose? Raise a child! Need motivation to take better care of yourself? Raise a child! Battling selfishness? Raise a child! It's the answer! *Michelle*

- October 1 -

God's Friendship

Can there be anything more wonderful than to experience the friendship of God? In Job 29:2-4 He says, *"Oh that I were in... the days when God preserved me; when His candle shined upon my head, and when by His light I walked through darkness... when the secret of God was upon my tabernacle."* The Hebrew word for "secret" is *sode,* which means "a couch, a cushion, a place where we share intimate friendship."

In other words, Job testified that he experienced the friendship of God lingering in his home. God was a familiar guest in his home.

Will you pray with me, "Dear Father, please come and make yourself at home in our home. I want your presence to linger with us throughout every day. Please expose anything that spoils your friendship in our home. Amen." *Nancy*

Are You Smiling at Your Husband?

Proverbs 12:4 says, *"A virtuous woman is a crown to her husband."*

A wife is truly a crown to her husband when she smiles her joy and affirmation to him! There is nothing he loves more than to see his wife smile. It is free and simple, yet makes such a huge marital impact.

My husband is so blessed by my smile. Why do I ever withhold it? *Michelle*

- October 2 -

What's Your Attitude?

Philippians 2:5 says, *"Let this mind be in you, which was also in Christ Jesus."* What is your attitude and mindset in your marriage relationship?

"I've got to look out for my life or no one else will!" Jesus, who was equal with God, laid down His Godhead and left the glory of heaven to become a man!

"My reputation is at stake!" Jesus made himself of no reputation.

"Why should I have to serve my husband? I have my own life." Jesus, who was God, became a servant.

"Why should I be the one to say 'Sorry' again?" Jesus humbled himself.

"Why do I have to submit?" Jesus was obedient to His Father to the point of death!

Will you let Him work His attitude in you? Read Philippians 2:5-8 and 1 Peter 4:1. *Nancy*

In His Palm

It is so comforting to know that we sit in the palm of God's very own hand (Isaiah 49:16). We don't need to know what tomorrow will bring or what our future holds. The Almighty will carry us all the way home. This gives me great comfort.

How supremely blessed we are to live with such peace! *Michelle*

- October 3 -

Things Come and Things Go

I love to speak positive statements. Another one of my affirmations is, "Things come and things go." When I wake up with a pain in some place in my body, rather than worrying or confessing my problem, I say, "Things come and things go."

May I give you a testimony? I have never had a problem in my body or a situation in my life that hasn't eventually gone away! When a difficulty arises, I'll repeat the same phrase rather than getting into a stew about it.

When you dwell on your problems, physical or emotional, they tend to become a part of you and only worsen. Don't immediately rush off to the doctor with every minor ache or pain. Instead, refuse to worry about it, don't confess it, give it some time, and you will often find it will disappear on its own! *Nancy*

Go to the Right Source

"Trust in the Lord with all thine heart; and lean not unto thine own understanding. In all thy ways acknowledge Him, and He shall direct thy paths" (Proverbs 3:5-6).

I need to heed this more often in the moments of my day. All too often I carry on in my own strength instead of going to the Source. This is not the best way to live. May God help us to live the best way! *Michelle*

- October 4 -

Trials Don't Last Forever

Can I pass on to you a very important piece of information? Trials don't go on forever! Even Job's suffering was not for a lifetime. No one knows how long he endured his trial, but he lived 140 years enjoying God's blessings after the trial. Some Talmudic information says it was for one year, yet another records it being seven years. Who knows, but it was not very long in a life of maybe 210 years!

Here is another important fact you must know. Your trial will not endure forever, but your God will! Psalm 9:7 says, *"The Lord shall endure forever."* You belong to a God who endures forever! Also read Psalm 102:12, 25-27 and Lamentations 5:19. *Nancy*

Huge Benefits

Today, I will try to show my husband that I respect his leadership and authority while I mother our children and keep our home. The benefits will be huge.

Doing things God's way always has the biggest payoffs! I know it can be difficult to implement at times. That's why we need each other, to urge one another on. So, let me encourage you today: keep doing it God's way—you're doing great. *Michelle*

- October 5 -

Power of Obedience

Romans 5:19 says, *"For as by one man's disobedience many were made sinners, so by the obedience of one shall many be made righteous."* What a powerful revelation! One moment of disobedience and the world and all future mankind was cursed with sin. And yet, because the Son of God was obedient to His Father's will, salvation is offered to all mankind. Only one act of disobedience and one act of obedience brought about world-changing and generation-changing impact!

What about our lives? When we willingly disobey God or even our husband, it not only affects our own life, but all those around us—even future generations. Conversely, one obedient decision can bring blessing to our current family as well as our future family.

May we always remember the far-reaching effect of disobeying or obeying. Are you blessing your family and future dynasties with obedient decisions? *Nancy*

You Are an Overcomer

You are doing an incredible job. Don't believe anyone that tells you any differently. Keep doing the awesome job you are doing and enjoy the journey. Every day you are a little more conformed into His image. Even in occasional defeat, you are still growing and overcoming. *Michelle*

- October 6 -

Be the Best Chef

"I'm a hopeless cook!"

"I hate cooking!"

I often hear women making these statements. May I encourage you to watch what comes out of your mouth? Don't confess negative statements. You bind yourself to your confession. As a mother and homemaker, cooking is part of your life! You may as well embrace it and speak positively about it.

I Peter 5:10 paints the picture of a woman who embraced her womanhood. The first thing she did was to raise children. The Greek word is *teknotropheo* and literally means to "feed and nourish children."

That means cooking for them! Why do it with a bad attitude? This is your profession—why not do it with joy? Release your creativity. Be the best chef. *Nancy*

Love in Action

I love watching a woman prepare meals for her family. It is a beautiful thing to prepare food.

When you peel, chop, and cut for your family, it is the furthest thing from drudgery. It is love in action, full of beauty and positive emotion. It speaks deeply of your care for your flock. *Michelle*

Wide As the Ocean

When Eve woke up to life, she was in her garden home. God had the home ready for her. This was to be her life. This is where she would bring life into the world and raise children to influence the world. This is where she would work and find fulfillment in all the gifts God had given her. It was not a place of restriction, but joy, freedom, and productivity. And this is His plan for you, dear mother. This is your life, too.

You are a *"keeper at home"* (Titus 2:5). Oops! That's not in the Bible, is it? Yes, it's still there, unless you cut it out. But, it is not restricting! Its vastness is as wide as the ocean and as high as the stars. The home is a birthing center, a mothering/nurturing center, a training and education center, a praise and worship center, a prayer center, an eating center, a cultural development center, a social center, a hospitality center, a counseling center, a health center, an industry center, a garden center, and a convalescent center! And this is just the beginning. *Nancy*

It's Love That Counts

What makes a believer truly godly? I was impacted today by the fact that you can have wisdom, knowledge, a strong prayer life, the respect of your church and neighbors, the most generous heart, a good marriage, and well-disciplined children, but if you lack love, you are truly lacking. Paul confessed, *"If I have all faith, so as to remove mountains, but do not have love, I am nothing"* I Corinthians 13:2 NASB). *Michelle*

- October 8 -

Feed Your Flock

Are you thinking about what to feed your family today? Sometimes, you wish you could forget about cooking meals! Be encouraged, dear mother, feeding your family is an important part of your mothering. Ezekiel 34:2 asks, *"Should not the shepherds feed the flocks?"*

It is the true shepherd that feeds his flock. It is the genuine shepherding mother who delights in preparing meals to feed her family. What are you planning to prepare for tonight's supper? *Nancy*

True Repentance

At our Canadian Thanksgiving table, we asked everyone to state three things they were thankful for that started with the first letter of their name. Everyone enjoyed it!

However, I was especially thankful this morning when my four-year-old son saw me fixing a picture frame he had carelessly broken yesterday. Unprompted, and with such sincerity, he looked into my eyes and said, "Mum, I sorry for breaking dat!"

Nothing melts our hearts, or the Lord's heart, more than heartfelt repentance! *Michelle*

- October 9 -

More Righteous Homes

My heart is burdened as I see evil encroaching more and more upon our land. My spirit rises up, and I want to push back the evil. I want righteousness to be established in the land. And yet, I feel insignificant against the darkness and deception that is increasing. What can we do? We must pray, of course.

However, I believe the greatest deterrent to evil is righteous families. Not fragmented families, but together-families. Homes where parents have caught the vision to not only feed and clothe their children, but to diligently train them to be soldiers of the cross. Homes where children are not sent out each day to be educated by a humanistic and socialistic agenda, but who are taught God's principles. Families who gather daily to pray and read God's Word together.

As the home is strengthened, the nation is strengthened. The more righteous the homes, the more righteousness will invade the nation! It's time for God-fearing families to arise. *"Arise, shine; for thy light is come, and the glory of the Lord is risen upon thee. For, behold, the darkness shall cover the earth, and gross darkness the people: but the Lord shall arise upon thee, and His glory shall be seen upon thee"* (Isaiah 60:1-2). *Nancy*

God Will Supply

My affirmation for today is that if God presents a task, He will supply everything needed to complete it! *Michelle*

- October 10 -

In Royal Service

Mother, your home is the place where you wield your greatest power. There is no other place where you can have more influence.

To be a mother at home with a little babe at your breast and teaching children gathered around your table is to have the honor and privilege of nurturing and molding lives for God who will one day determine the destiny of the nation.

Lift up your eyes, dear mother. Don't let society deceive you. You are in royal service. You are working for the King of kings. You could not be doing anything greater. *Nancy*

It's a Great Work

You are doing a GREAT work! Don't let the enemy use discouragement to prevent you from the amazing work you are doing. You are building your family and leaving a godly heritage. This is the greatest work in which you can be involved. Keep it up. *Michelle*

A Home of Wonder

God wants your home to be a welcoming place—a home where you welcome His presence, where you welcome the babies He wondrously gives to you, and where you welcome people in hospitality. He wants your home to be filled with worship, wisdom, warmth, and wellbeing. He wants your home to be filled with wonder—the divine wonder of a precious newborn arriving in your home.

The wonder of the heavenly atmosphere that comes with a baby fresh from God cannot be duplicated. You delight in the wonder of watching your baby's first smile, his first laugh, his first word, and his first steps. You look on in wonder as you watch your children grow into mature adults and fulfill the gifts and destiny that God has planned for them.

Truly, the home is a wonderful, wonder-filled place. *Nancy*

The Normal Abnormal

We all receive negative comments from time to time, but what a pleasure it is to hear a positive comment. One of my all-time favorites was when a gentleman heard me speak at a homeschool conference about my life with 11 children.

He told me, "You make the abnormal seem normal!"

Thank you, Lord. *Michelle*

- October 12 -

Unpopular Words

Yield! Submit! Obey! Unpopular words. Why do we cringe from them? Is it because they are the opposite to our fleshly way of living?

And yet, they belong to God's kingdom. They are the vocabulary of God's kingdom. We are chosen for the purpose of obedience to Jesus Christ. We are sanctified by obedience to the truth (1 Peter 1:2, 14, 22). We cannot be changed into the image of Christ except by obedience. We are either *"obedient children"* (1 Peter 1:14) or *"disobedient children"* (Ephesians 2:2).

To walk in obedience to God, to the truth in His Word, and to our husband, is proof that we belong to the kingdom of God. To walk disobediently reveals that we are still living in the devil's kingdom. *Nancy*

No Need to Panic

One of Nancy's sayings is, "Sarah's daughters do not panic." This is good to recall when the stress is high!

What good will panic do? We needn't fear. We are the daughters of God, and He will see us through! *Michelle*

- October 13 -

Think Oneness

Created in the image of God, you were created for oneness. God's plan is for you to be ONE with your husband. It is His very first principle for marriage (Genesis 2:24). You are to be first of all *"one flesh,"* but also one in spirit, mind, heart, and purpose.

Of course, you may be tempted to be independent, but don't give into that spirit. That's what Satan wants. He is intent on destroying and undermining all God's plans. Independence brought Satan to destruction; it will bring you and your marriage to destruction, too.

God's plan of oneness leads to blessing and life. Think oneness. *Nancy*

Celebrate Your Marriage

Why not celebrate your marriage today? Dress up, have a special meal, have a passionate, lingering kiss, and speak some affirming words that may have been neglected. Join together in oneness if that has been neglected, too. Build on your marital relationship. *Michelle*

- October 14 -

Food, Not a Snack

What is your food? Jesus said, *"My food is to do the will of Him who sent Me and to accomplish His work"* (John 4:34 NASB). In other words, it was His life's passion to fulfill the will of God.

What is God's will for your life? To embrace motherhood and to train your children for God on His behalf! Make it your passion. Delight in it (Psalm 40:7-8). Make it your food instead of a scant snack! *Nancy*

Toss Trinkets, but Not Relationships

Today, I finally let go of a sentimental trinket that has been broken and glued back together countless times over the last 20 plus years. After all, it really isn't that important. Yet, I have tried time and time again to keep it functioning and on my shelf, despite several moves, falls, and breaks.

I was shocked to realize that all the effort I put into fixing my item is often not even put into valuable relationships! Many around me give up on their marriage or rebellious young people because of the pain, hassle, and effort involved. I was almost one of them regarding my own marriage years ago! Yet, tossing these relationships out is very detrimental on so many fronts.

Why do we pour lots of loving attention on things of little value, yet give up on the major things? We must not give up, and we must encourage those around us to not give up either. Nurture, encourage, and develop your precious relationships—and watch them bloom. Toss your trinkets, but do not toss your God-given relationships! *Michelle*

- October 15 -

Champion the Truth

I have this quote written in front of my journal. "Truth can never win unless it is promulgated. Truth does not carry within itself an antitoxin to falsehood. The cause of truth must be championed, and it MUST BE CHAMPIONED DYNAMICALLY" (William F. Buckley, Jr.).

Paul *"expounded and testified the kingdom of God, persuading them concerning Jesus, both out of the law of Moses, and out of the prophets, from morning till evening. And some believed the things which were spoken, and some believed not"* (Acts 28:23-24).

It is not our responsibility who believes; it is our responsibility to proclaim the truth. The outcome is in God's hands, but we can be encouraged that there will also be some who will believe. His Word never returns without accomplishing its purpose (Isaiah 55:11). *Nancy*

Attitudes are Catchy

Part of being a helpmate is inspiring your husband to turn his heart toward God, home, and children. One of the most practical ways to do this is to enjoy your faith, home, and all your children immensely.

When a husband comes home to a wife that complains about her home life and is always frustrated as a mother, he naturally wants to lessen her grief. If he sees that her faith, home life, and children are bringing her great joy, he will be much more likely to embrace what she embraces. Attitudes are catchy! Your attitude is the best way to influence and bless your husband and others! *Michelle*

- October 16 -

God's Balances

Are you going through a heavy trial? It seems like it is going on forever! I know this is how it feels to you, but may I ask you to put your troubles in God's balances? Now things look a little different.

God says in II Corinthians 4:17, *"For our light affliction, which is but for a moment, worketh for us a far more exceeding and eternal weight of glory."* It seems as though you can't come out from under it, but God says it is *"momentary."* It feels so heavy to you, but in the light of eternity it is a *"light"* affliction.

There are more blessings yet. God says that your trial, if you let God work His grace in you, is producing rewards in heaven for you. He uses five adjectives to describe the glory you will receive. Your trials are working for you a 1) *far,* 2) *more,* 3) *exceeding,* 4) *eternal,* and 5) *weight of glory.* It will make all your present troubles seem like nothing. You can rejoice! *Nancy*

They Long for Respect

Our minister discussed how wives need to respect their husbands, even when they don't feel like it. Many times husbands have their confidence shaken and their leadership thwarted by the words, attitudes, and actions of their wives—wives who should respect them because God said to. Good, but painful, reminder.

As a wife, you have incredible power to influence your husband. *Michelle*

Hold on!

One of the things John the Apostle saw in his vision on the Isle of Patmos was the souls who were *"slain because of the Word of God, and because of the testimony which they had maintained"* (Revelation 6:9 NASB). I am challenged by the word "maintained." These martyrs held onto the truth. They were faithful. They didn't give up when the going got tough, and they faced persecution and even death.

Do our children see us maintaining our faith, even in the midst of difficult trials? Are we teaching them to hold onto truth, no matter what the circumstances? Are we preparing them to know how to stand in the future, in times that may not be as easy as we enjoy now? *Nancy*

Start Now!

This day is a gift. How will you spend yours? Make the most of each moment as you serve God in all of the ordinary tasks in your home.

Leave your mark on this day with a positive, joy-filled attitude. Start right now by giving someone a great big hug! *Michelle*

- October 18 -

Lean On Your Beloved

The children of Israel came into the wilderness complaining, independent, and wanting their own way. And, watch out if they didn't get it! But, they came out of the wilderness dependent upon their God.

Sometimes we have to go through a wilderness experience to realize that hanging onto our independence only ends in destruction. We learn that God's way is the way that works. It works in daily life. It works in our marriage relationship. The sooner we learn this lesson in our lives, the better it will be for ourselves and everyone around us.

Song of Solomon 8:5 is a beautiful picture of the bride of Christ and also of our individual marriage, *"Who is this that cometh up from the wilderness, **leaning upon her beloved**." Nancy*

Growing Through Trials

Life comes fraught with trials and few remain untouched by them. However, we have the tools to carry us through! When we are in the depths, God tenderly upholds us. We are molded more into His image, and we come out softer and wiser on the other end. When we support others who are struggling, the love of Christ flows through us, and we grow through the trial. Don't despair in the hard times. *Michelle*

- October 19 -

The Little Things

Are you dreaming of doing great things for God? Start with the little things. Is your laundry up to date? Are your dishes done and your counters wiped?

But you want to be involved in this mission or that organization! Again, what about the little things? Are you faithfully mothering your children and preparing meals for your husband and family?

Before God gave Moses the enormous mission of delivering the Israelites from Egypt and leading them through the desert, He first sent him out to the backside of the desert to look after a few sheep!

Before David rose to become king of Israel, he looked after the sheepfold and the ewes *"great with young"* (Psalm 78:71-72).

Any anointed ministry that you will ever do will be an extension of your mothering. We can't get away from God's principle of *"He that is faithful in that which is least is faithful also in much"* (Luke 16:10). *Nancy*

The Biggest Impact

Speaking of little things, they often carry the biggest impact. A kind word, a gentle answer, a huge smile, a warm hug, a sincere compliment, a quick prayer, a tiny favor, a spontaneous act of kindness, a selfless gesture, a small token of appreciation, an encouraging word, a listening ear, and a good laugh.

As we offer these blessings, we in turn are richly blessed. *Michelle*

- October 20 -

Close Up the Cracks

You as a mother have the responsibility to guard the gates of your home. Your husband may sit in the city gates, but you sit in the seat of the home gates. Look out for any encroacher who tries to bring deception or evil into your home! They'll have to face you first!

We are told in Proverbs 14:19, *"The evil bow before the good; and the wicked at the gates of the righteous."* The Amplified version reads, *"uncompromisingly righteous."*

As you stand, uncompromisingly, against evil in your home and at the gates of your home, you can expect the wicked to bow before you. But take note, the wicked will detect any compromise or weakening of your convictions. This makes a crack for him to enter your home. Make sure there are no cracks. *Nancy*

One Day at a Time

"We can easily manage if we will only take each day, the burden appointed to it. But, the load will be too heavy for us if we carry yesterday's burden over again today and then add the burden of the morrow before we are required to bear it" (John Newton).

I like this quote, except I try not to think of daily loads, no matter how heavy, as burdens. I look upon them as opportunities in the grand adventure of life! *Michelle*

- October 21 -

Love Life

Did you know that God wants us to love life? He doesn't only give us life, but abundant life (John 10:10). If we want to *"love life and see good days,"* I Peter 3:10-11 gives us the secret. It gives four principles to make it happen:

> *1) Keep your tongue from evil.* Notice that God doesn't say He will keep it from evil, but that **you** must "refrain" and stop your tongue from saying the wrong thing. Of course, God will help you as you cry out to Him.
>
> *2) Keep your lips from speaking deceit.*
>
> *3) Turn away from evil and do good.* The Greek word is *ekklino* which means, "to shun, to decline, to go out of the way to avoid evil."
>
> *4) Seek peace and pursue it.* Especially in the home, which means we will often need to humble ourselves to keep the peace.

I love the paraphrase of the Message Bible, *"Say nothing evil or hurtful; snub evil and cultivate good; run after peace for all you're worth."* Teach your children these secrets. *Nancy*

Keep Focused

Another day the Lord has made for us! Time to focus again on our important building work—building up our husband, our children, our faith, and our homes. Sometimes we have to do some tearing down first; tearing down our pride, bitterness and selfishness! *Michelle*

- October 22 -

The Best Curriculum

There are so many books and curriculums available to help us teach our children. Often we get bewildered in knowing which one to use. But the best training manual is the Scriptures.

II Timothy 3:16-17 NASB tells us, *"All Scripture is inspired by God and profitable for teaching, for reproof, for correction, for training in righteousness; so that the man of God may be adequate, equipped for every good work."*

We know this, of course, but how much time do we spend teaching our children from the Scriptures? It is the Scriptures, more than any other book, that prepares our children for life and success. *Nancy*

Maximize the Moments

The exciting thing about life is that we never really know what a day will hold. Maximize the moments you have today. Fill them with love and service. Create the atmosphere you want in your home.

Happy loving service today! *Michelle*

- October 23 -

Keep Your Cool

Do you find it easy to "keep your cool"? It's not too easy, is it? Yet, this quality is very precious to God. I Peter 3:4 says, *"Let it be the hidden man of the heart, in that which is not corruptible, even the ornament of a meek (gentle) and quiet spirit, which is in the sight of God of great price."*

The word "quiet" is *hesuchios* in the Greek and it literally means "to keep one's seat"! In other words, when your feathers are ruffled and your children are getting on your nerves, instead of lashing out in anger and "blowing your cool," you keep calm. Don't jump off the seat of your emotions and get into the flesh. Stay rested.

"Help!" you cry. "How do you do that?"

By the power of Christ. He lives in a state of rest, and He lives in you. Let Him live His life through you. *Nancy*

I'll Keep My Job

My 10-year-old daughter, Havenne, feeds her baby sister breakfast. I suggested that we pass her job down to her younger sister, Jilissa. She said, "That is my job! Maybe Jilissa can do the next baby! Solana is mine!"

I sure hope there is a "next" baby. Obviously, so does Havenne! *Michelle*

Accept His Will

We talked yesterday about having a "quiet" spirit. It also means "to bear with tranquility the difficulties we face in life and relationships." Many times, we live in a state of turmoil instead of tranquility because we resist the yoke. We hold onto our stubborn spirit of wanting our own way. To yield to the yoke, and accept your situation, will bring restfulness to your spirit. I love Hannah Hurnard's words...

> *In acceptance lieth peace,*
> *O my heart be still;*
> *Let thy restless worries cease*
> *And accept His will.*
> *Though this test be not thy choice,*
> *It is His—therefore rejoice.*
>
> *Cease from sighs and murmuring,*
> *Sing His loving grace,*
> *This thing means thy furthering*
> *To a wealthy place.*
> *From thy fears He'll give release,*
> *In acceptance lieth peace.*

Nancy

Mommy Eyes

I feel very thankful for the gift of "mommy eyes." Do you have them, too? At times they seem to be the only ones able to locate things! Praise the Lord that I am so needed in my family. *Michelle*

What Sacrifice?

Talking together about motherhood with a few women recently, one mother said, "Oh it's so hard. It's such a sacrifice!"

Immediately, my daughter Evangeline, piped up, "What are you sacrificing?"

When we confess that motherhood is a sacrifice, we imply that there is something better we could be doing, and we had to give it up for the sake of motherhood! That is a lie.

Motherhood is the highest calling God has given to us. It is our LIFE. It may be challenging, but any worthwhile career is challenging. I think we are programmed by society to think that it is a sacrifice.

We need our minds renewed to God's way of thinking, to think truth instead of deception. *Nancy*

Not an Inconvenience

I read a quote from Kittie Franz, "Remember, you are not managing an inconvenience; you are raising a human being."

This message should be propagated around the world. The cultural view of children is so much less than how God defines and values children in Scripture. I believe that there is no greater way to spend one's time than to impact another life for the glory of God. *Michelle*

Which Company?

Psalm 107:41 says that God *"maketh Him families like a flock."* God delights in a flock. That speaks of not one sheep, but many. But here God is talking about families. He delights to give families many children if they will let Him. Isn't it sad that the majority of Christians spurn large families?

What is the right reaction? Verses 42-43 say, *"The righteous shall see it, and rejoice; and all iniquity shall stop her mouth. Whoso is wise, and will observe these things, even they shall understand the lovingkindness of the Lord."*

The Bible states that when the righteous see God giving a couple another baby, they rejoice! They don't say cutting remarks or ask, "Don't you know how to prevent that?" The Scripture tells us that the wise understand that each new baby is a blessing from God and comes from *"the lovingkindness of the Lord."* Are we in the "righteous" and "wise" company who rejoice? Whose side are we on? *Nancy*

Words of Wisdom

I love listening and learning from those a stage ahead of me in life. What a privilege it is when we glean from our elders. One of the grandmothers that attends my church shared with me something I haven't forgotten. She said, "Isn't it something how $20.00 seems so little in the shopping mall and yet so large in the church offering?" I love her! *Michelle*

- October 27 -

Where Is Your Heart?

Psalm 113:4-6 describes God as, *"High above all nations, and His glory above the heavens."* He is so high that He has to stoop down to look upon heaven and earth.

After expressing the greatness of God, you would think the psalmist would then list some of His mighty acts. But no, He reveals the true heart of our God who dwells on high. Verses 7-9 tell us that *"He raiseth the poor out of the dust, and lifts up the needy out of the dunghill... He maketh the barren woman to keep house, and to be a joyful mother of children."*

What is closest to the heart of our great God who has to humble himself to look upon the earth? He loves the poor and the mother in her home with her little children. This is where God's heart is focused.

What is the focus of your heart? *Nancy*

Sweet and True

The best gifts in life are free. One of my favorites is when a sweaty, grubby little son of mine proudly strolls in with a handful of plucked weeds, maybe a blossom thrown in, and says, "Look Mummy, flowers for you!"

Such love is consistently found on this earth—sweet and true, unconditional, accepting, and forgiving—in the hearts of precious children. *Michelle*

- October 28 -

Return to Your Rest

How easy it is to get out of a state of rest. Instead of allowing Christ to have His way in our lives, we take control. That's the easiest way to get into a state of anxiety. But why strive when you can abide?

We need to confess the words of the psalmist in Psalm 116:7, *"Return unto thy rest, O my soul."* When you start to get agitated, speak these words out loud! Yes, out loud! Your spirit will hear and get in line. You might want to print these words and pin them up in your kitchen as a constant reminder. I love the words from John Greenleaf Whittier's hymn…

> *Drop Thy still dews of quietness,*
> *Till all our strivings cease;*
> *Take from our souls the strain and stress,*
> *And let our ordered lives confess*
> *The beauty of Thy peace.*

Nancy

Complaining Hurts the Ears

Complaining! We all do it, often without even thinking about it. When we complain, we do a lot more than simply express ourselves. Complaining not only gives us a negative mind frame, which is bad enough, but it also creates insecurity in those that hear it. They often feel they have failed us and have somehow contributed to our unhappiness. That is not the message I want to give. I want those around me to know they enhance my life and bring me joy.

"Put a guard over my mouth, O Lord!" *Michelle*

- October 29 -

Can You Be Sure?

It is a grief to see young people turn away from the Lord. Mothers sometimes ask me "How can I be sure that my children will continue to walk with the Lord?" Let me share a fact with you. It is only the *"unstable"* who will turn away. II Peter 2:14 talks about deceivers who go about *"beguiling **unstable** souls."*

As parents, we must do all we can to make sure our children are stable in the faith. It is our responsibility to faithfully impart God's Word to our children morning and evening, as we sit in our homes and as we walk along the way. We must teach them biblical doctrines, answer their questions, and model a life of sincere faith before them. We pray that God will give them hearts to understand and embrace that faith; we pray that they will not be fickle, but fixed upon Christ; we pray that they will not be vacillators, but valiant for the truth. It is our goal to make sure they are rooted and grounded in the faith so they will be unmoved! *Nancy*

Counteract the Lies

Taking every thought captive to the obedience of Christ is not only about stopping sinful thoughts, but also the lies that we believe—the lies that tell us we don't measure up, we're not good enough, talented enough, beautiful enough, or smart enough, etc. These must be counteracted with the truth that we have everything in Christ and can do all things through Him (Philippians 4:13). *Michelle*

- October 30 -

Who Are We?

Calling upon the Lord defines that we are the people of God. Psalm 99:6 NASB says, *"Moses and Aaron were among His priests, and Samuel was among those who called on His name; they called upon the Lord and He answered them."*

The early Christians were known as those who called upon the name of the Lord. Could we be called this today? You may like to check out a few Scriptures regarding this subject—Genesis 25:26; Exodus 14:15; 15:25; I Samuel 7:9; 12:18; 22:4-5 and Jeremiah 10:25; Acts 9:14, 21; 22:16; Romans 10:13; I Corinthians 1:2 and II Timothy 2:22.

Are you a mother who calls upon the Lord? Do you run to God rather than man? Is your family known as a family who calls upon the Lord? Would they come to you if they needed prayer?

I am sure that when families and the church of God begin to call upon the name of the Lord that we will see God's hand move in mighty ways. *Nancy*

Unbelievable

Three of my children were discussing how sweet babies are. One said, "Surprising that people give away babies!" I told them that some people do things to their bodies to prevent having babies.

She looked at me in astonishment and questioned, "On purpose?" Oh, to see things through the eyes of a child! *Michelle*

- October 31 -

Look Up!

Where are your eyes focused? On the earthly or on the eternal? On your problem or on the Lord? It's much easier to see the earthly, as that's what we see right in front of us. However, things get into perspective when we see them from an eternal purpose.

II Corinthians 4:18 says, *"We look not at the things which are seen, but at the things which are not seen: for the things which are seen are temporal; but the things which are not seen are eternal."*

Let's look at things from God's point of view. Our problems seem daunting in front of us; but, in the light of eternity, they are only temporary! Get your eyes off them and onto the "real" world. Set your eyes on what you cannot see, not on what you can see! *Nancy*

An Attitude of Gratitude

There are so many ways to look at things. Why not look at them with joy and gratitude? It takes just as much effort, but has more benefits.

Today, by the grace of God, I will resist the urge to complain. How about you? I know He will help us. *Michelle*

- November 1 -

Filled First

"Then Peter, filled with the Holy Spirit, said unto them..." (Acts 4:8)

Wouldn't it be a good idea to be filled with the Holy Spirit before we spouted off with our mouth? It would save a lot of heartache for ourselves and our family, wouldn't it?

No wonder the Greek tense of Ephesians 5:18 means, *"Be ye, being filled with the Holy Spirit"*—continuous present tense! We need to constantly rely on the Holy Spirit. *Nancy*

Why Do I Complain?

"How great is the love the Father has lavished on us, that we should be called children of God" (1 John 3:1 NIV).

We serve a Sovereign Lord that knows and controls all from beginning to end and we are His. When I ponder this reality, I am humbled. Why do I ever complain or worry? We could not possibly be in better Hands. Silly me! *Michelle*

Eating in God's Presence

I love reading about the wonderful time when Jethro, Moses, and Aaron and the elders of Israel ate together *"in the presence of God"* (Exodus 18:12 NIV). What an amazing experience!

But did you know that God wants us to eat all our meals together in His presence? God has chosen the blessedness of eating together to bring His presence into our home. And yet, how frequently we allow "lesser" things to hinder us from this blessing. It seems that the enemy makes sure that extracurricular activities and sports are during the time of family meal times.

All these things are good, but let's watch that we are not robbed of what is the best! *Nancy*

Table Bonding

The family meal table is important for so many reasons. It unites each family member regardless of age. Everyone feels a part of the table. It brings unity and anticipation to every member.

Today, we are having a special meal to honor my husband, and everyone from young to old is excited. I love the bonding at the table! *Michelle*

- November 3 -

God Willing

Are you making plans to move or go here or there? Growing up as a child in my church community, it was familiar to hear the words, D.V, the shortened version for the Latin phrase, God Willing.

The message comes from James 4:13-16 NASB, *"Come now, you who say, 'Today or tomorrow we will go to such and such a city, and spend a year there and engage in business and make a profit.' Yet you do not know what your life will be like tomorrow... Instead, you ought to say, 'If the Lord wills, we will live and also do this or that.'"*

Of course, we have to make plans. We have to get moving, just as Abraham's servant confessed, *"I being in the way, the Lord led me"* (Genesis 24:27). But, as we make plans and move along, we are totally open to God changing our direction and steering us into His ultimate plan. *Nancy*

Love When Impossible

A true test of character is to shine when things are dark, to love when it seems impossible, and to exercise self-control when things feel out of control. Thankfully, by God's grace, we are able to accomplish these things. Keep looking to Him and leaning on Him. *Michelle*

- November 4 -

Omnipotent Comforter

Even though the Most High God is high above the heavens and high above all kings and rulers, yet He bends down to the poor and the lowly. We see a picture of this in Psalm 91:1, *"He that dwelleth in the secret place of the MOST HIGH (El Elyon) shall abide under the shadow of the ALMIGHTY (El Shaddai)."*

In one little Scripture we see the opposites of God's character linked as one. El Elyon, the Omnipotent Potentate of the universe is also El Shaddai, the "breasted one" who is full of mercy and always available to comfort, nurture, and protect us.

Psalm 138:6 says, *"Though the Lord be high, yet hath He respect unto the lowly."* Also read Psalm 113.

As you experience the awe of your great God, teach your children to understand who He is, too. *Nancy*

Make Good Memories

Enjoy your flock today, sweet mother. Smile as often as you can, even in the tough moments. Things will go much smoother. Make good memories today! Thankfully, our attitudes can make a significant impact on the outcome of the day. *Michelle*

- November 5 -

Throw Out the Trash

You are commissioned to be part of a great building program—the building and strengthening of your family. There is no greater building program, because building individual families builds the nation and continuing generations.

However, you can't effectively build if there is rubbish in the way. When they were building the wall in Nehemiah's day, they complained that they couldn't continue building the wall because there was so much rubble to be moved (Nehemiah 4:10). Do you have rubbish in piling up in your home (not just literal trash, but sin and hindrances that grieve the Holy Spirit)?

Stop. Don't continue living this way any longer. Ask God to help you deal with this rubbish. Talk to your family about it and **all get involved in the clean up**! Throw out anything and everything that hinders your great building program. *Nancy*

Joy Robber

Isn't it amazing how fast grumpiness can steal joy out of the home? I must admit that I let this affect me all too often! It is better to realize that time is very precious, and that I cannot get it back once it is spent. Knowing this day will never come again helps me guard against joy robbing! I am focusing on my blessings instead. How about you? *Michelle*

Lighter Shopping Cart

We constantly hear about de-cluttering our homes, but have you thought about de-cluttering your shopping cart? It's amazing how much we can eliminate and save money.

Next time you go shopping, may I suggest that you read all labels? When you see sugar, corn syrup, red color (and all the other colors which are cancer forming), or any words in the ingredient list that are too difficult to pronounce, put the item back on the shelf! Fast!

Throw back all packaged, processed, and de-vitalized products. Keep mainly to the produce aisle and buy whole foods, instead. *Nancy*

Disarm Your Husband

My plan today is to disarm my husband with a very passionate kiss. This will not be the typical goodnight kiss or the "see you after work" kiss, but rather a kiss that says, "You're the one I want today and forever!" I bet it will be amazing what that one little kiss will do!

Make a plan, get excited about it, and fan the flame of your marriage! *Michelle*

- November 7 -

Restore Relationships

Do you, like me, long for the *"restoration of all things,"* the time when God will subdue all wickedness and bring everything, everyone, and all nations into subjection to Christ?

Or, perhaps you are longing for restoration of situations that are nearer to hand. There are relationships in your family and extended family that need restoring. The final restoration is coming, but God is also restoring now. He is the God of restoration and wants to heal estranged relationships.

Don't ever give up. Keep praying. Ask God to show you how you can break down barriers and walls. Ask Him to give you a soft heart and forgiving spirit. He needs you to be involved in the restoration. He wants you to be *"the restorer of paths to dwell in"* (Isaiah 58: 12). *Nancy*

God Is Working in You!

"God the Father chose you long ago, and the Spirit has made you holy. As a result, you have obeyed Jesus Christ and are cleansed by His blood" (1 Peter 1:2 NLT).

You have been chosen by God, you are cleansed by the blood of Jesus Christ, and you are made holy through the sanctifying work of the Holy Spirit. And God continues to work in you by His Spirit, *"For God is working in you, giving you the desire to obey Him and the power to do what pleases Him"* (Philippians 2:13 NLT). The Holy Spirit is equipping you daily for your task. *Michelle*

- November 8 -

Fear God Rather Than Man

Nehemiah tells us in Nehemiah 5:15 that he refrained from doing certain things that others felt free to do because *"of the fear of God."* Rather than the standard of the people around him (even governors), Nehemiah based his lifestyle on the fear of God. He wasn't content to live like the status quo.

How do you and your family live? Teach your children, by example, to make every decision in the light of the fear of God. Inspire in them the courage to fear God rather than man. *Nancy*

Working Together

Where I live, the Canadian geese are flocking together as they prepare to head south. They effortlessly group together and fill the sky as they look out for one another. So it is with believers. We are one big body, working together for the glory of the Father and the edification of the saints.

Romans 14:19 says, *"Let us therefore follow after the things which make for peace, and things wherewith one may edify another."*

I love being a part of Christ's body. I love that after I fall, I can repent and feel clean, renewed, and ready to be used in the body again. It is a wonderful life! *Michelle*

- November 9 -

Can We Discern?

It was a beautiful sunrise this morning. I love to see the red sky silhouetted against the bare trees of winter. Isn't it amazing that we can discern weather patterns and yet not understand the times?

Jesus said in Luke 12:56, *"Ye hypocrites, ye can discern the face of the sky and of the earth; but how is it that ye do not discern this time?"*

Jesus was speaking to the Israelites who missed the most important event in history. Their Messiah was living amongst them and they did not recognize Him!

How easy it is to miss divine revelation if we don't stay close to the Lord. It does not come by intellect, but by the revelation of the Holy Spirit. May we be like the tribe of Issachar who *"had understanding of the times, to know what Israel ought to do."* (I Chronicles 12:32) *Nancy*

New Habits

My 10-year-old daughter asked, "Mum, how do I get rid of a habit? I don't want to do it, but I DO it!"

That's so true for us all, isn't it? Doing what we do not want to do. I told her to make a conscious effort to stop every time she catches herself, and soon a new habit can form. I think I'll work on making some positive changes, too. The Lord is our strength and help. Motivation and victory can be ours. *Michelle*

- November 10 -

Fold Your Flock

When Jesus spoke to Peter after His resurrection, He exhorted him three times, *"Feed My lambs... Feed My sheep... Feed My sheep"* (John 21:15-17). The first and last exhortation to "feed" literally means to feed. However, the second time Jesus said these words, He used a different word, *polmaino*, which means the whole office of the shepherd—guiding, guarding, tending, feeding, folding the flock, and leading them to nourishment.

In biblical times the shepherd folded his flock each night. He counted each one and made sure they were all in the fold, safe and secure from any wild beasts. During the day, he watched over them constantly with his rod and staff and led them to green pastures.

God has also made you a shepherdess as you fold your flock. Your work is very precious to His Shepherd's heart. *Nancy*

God Has the Solutions

Today, I have had lots of practice taking every thought captive. Instead of dwelling on my problems, I've made an effort to focus on the One who has all the solutions! I have to continually remind myself to place all of my fears, concerns, hurts, and incompetencies as a wife and mother at the foot of the cross.

Every time I do, He grants me complete and utter peace. In addition, taking every thought captive keeps me in a constant state of prayer. How are your thoughts today? *Michelle*

- November 11 -

The Lord Most High

The youth of our current age (and perhaps adults, too) are besotted with the fascination of media and technology. Wherever you look, people sit behind a laptop or their eyes are glued to their iphone or ipad.

Does this take away our wonder and awe of the **MOST** HIGH GOD? Psalm 47:2 says, *"The LORD MOST HIGH is terrible; He is a great King over all the earth."*

He is Potentate, Ruler, Sovereign and the Supreme Being of the universe. He should capture our attention and the amazement and awe of our children.

Do I acknowledge Him as the Most High in my life? Does He rule in every decision and situation? Do we function as a family with the awareness that He is Ruler over all? What a difference this would make in our family life. *Nancy*

Family Oriented Cultures

I love traveling to other cultures and realizing that most other cultures appreciate large families. I met a young man today in Costa Rica that hopes to marry one day and have 11 children. That is so refreshing. Rarely is that sentiment seen or heard of in North America! *Michelle*

- November 12 -

Breathe Truth

It's the twelfth day of the month, and I was reading Proverbs 12 in the Amplified version. Verse 17 says, *"He who breathes out truth shows forth righteousness."*

I was interested to read that he *"breathes out"* truth. I checked it in the Strong's Concordance, and yes, it is absolutely correct! The Hebrew, *puach*, means "to breathe, to puff." We breathe without thinking; it is completely natural to us.

May we become so filled with truth that we breathe it out unconsciously. Every time we open our mouths, may we speak truth and godly wisdom. Amen. *Nancy*

Step Out in Faith

I don't want to have faith without love. Therefore, today I will smile, hug, kiss, cuddle, and find things to verbally praise in my husband and children, even if I don't feel like it!

It is a beautiful thing to not be bossed around by my feelings. It is a powerful thing to have the Spirit of God enabling me to love others. It is just a matter of stepping out in faith and doing it. James 2:20 says, "Faith without works is dead." *Michelle*

- November 13 -

Shine More Brightly

Jesus said in John 9:5, *"As long as I am in the world, I am the light of the world."* Because Jesus lives in me and you, we can also confess, "As long as I live in this world, I will be a light to the world."

Be a light to your family today. You couldn't be doing anything more powerful.

Proverbs 6:23 says that our teaching is a light to our children that will continue to mold them through life—to lead them as they walk, keep them as they sleep, and talk with them when they are awake, so they will be kept from evil.

Don't let the light fade, but keep shining more brightly the longer you live. Proverbs 4:18 says, *"The path of the just is as the shining light, that shineth **more and more** unto the perfect day."* Nancy

Snuff Out Self Pity

To rise above self-pity is to love others regardless of their treatment of us. Self-pity stifles this because the focus is on our own wounds. The grace of God enables us to see that we are no less sinful than the ones who hurt us and therefore we can rise above self-pity and love even those that seem most difficult! Praise God for His strength in us! *Michelle*

A Straight Path

In Mathew 3:3, John the Baptist cried out, *"Prepare ye the way of the Lord, make His paths straight."*

The paths of the Lord are straight paths. No crooked paths on God's highway! To make a way for the Lord in our life and in our family, we must turn from every crooked and deviating path.

Ask the Lord to keep you and your children on a straight path. *Nancy*

The Icing On the Cake

We recently attended my cousin's wedding, and at one point she said to her new husband, "I don't promise that everything will always be perfect, but I do promise to be the icing on your cake because the icing is the best part." I loved that.

I want to be the icing on my husband's cake, too! I want to be the best part of his day, the best part of his life. This is a high calling that takes immense effort, but the payoff is huge.

A strong, loving relationship impacts not only our own marriage, but the marriages of our children, grandchildren, and great-grandchildren. It even affects friends, neighbors, and others who may be watching our example.

"Father, please help me to be the sweet icing on my husband's cake, every single day! Amen." *Michelle*

- November 15 -

Hotter and Hotter

Jesus said in Matthew 24:12-13, *"Because iniquity shall abound, the love of many shall wax cold. But he that shall endure to the end, the same shall be saved."*

When wickedness encroaches upon us, many are sucked into deception and evil. May God help you and your children to stand against the deceptions of evil in this present age.

Instead of getting colder, press into God and His truth and become hotter and hotter! Never allow yourself or your family to be "luke-warm" (Revelation 3:15-16). *Nancy*

Give Time and Energy

We live in a world that does not respect the institution of marriage. Instead of letting that get us down, let us use it as fuel to build up our marriage.

There is nothing like a bit of extra motivation to help us see how precious our marriage is and how worthy it is of our time and energy.

Make the most of every opportunity to enjoy the oneness that God ordained you to experience in your marriage in the emotional, intellectual, spiritual, and physical realms. *Michelle*

- November 16 -

God Loves Order

God told Aaron and his sons to keep the tabernacle *"in order from evening to morning before the Lord continually"* (Exodus 27:21 and Leviticus 24:3). God wanted His place of residence kept in order!

Does your home belong to the Lord? He wants it to be kept in order, too. I know it's not easy when you have little ones messing up all day, but you will be more motivated when you know you are pleasing the Lord.

I love the words, *"before the Lord."* See yourself doing everything in your home before the eyes of the Lord. Schedule "clean up" times at regular intervals throughout the day, and especially before your husband arrives home in the evening. *Nancy*

Christ Is My Strength

"I can do all things through Christ who strengthens me" (Philippians 4:13). Let's walk in this truth, even if our feelings tell us otherwise!

We can do all things. Not maybe, not perhaps, not once in a while or sometimes. He promises to strengthen us for ALL tasks that we face! *Michelle*

- November 17 -

God Is With You In the Night

An *Above Rubies* reader wrote to me, "I was thinking how Anna, the prophetess, could fast day and night (Luke 2:36-37). How did she fast at night? And then it hit me. When I am up at night with the baby or little ones with bad dreams, wet beds, or sick tummies, I can look upon it as 'fasting from sleep.' As I do this unto the Lord, it will be a little more bearable."

God is with you as you tend to your little ones at night, dear mother. Instead of feeling frustrated, let Him wrap His loving arms around you.

And when possible, take your baby back to bed with you. Your baby will be much happier, and you'll both be able to sleep. *Nancy*

We Love Specials

Who doesn't love a "special"? "More for less," "Two for one," "Buy one, get one free." We are applauded, even envied, when we take advantage of such deals.

But why is there little applause when a mother wants twins or if we adopt "challenged" children? Often mothers are pitied because of the work involved, instead of being applauded. It is all backwards.

Children, blessings that come straight from the hand of the Lord, will certainly be provided for. We can be sure of that. *Michelle*

- November 18 -

Cheerful Gatherings

At harvest time, God told the children of Israel to bring the first of the crops, place them before the Lord, and worship Him. Then He told them, *"Go home to feast on all the good things He has given thee, with all thy household, with Levite and wanderer that are thy neigbours"* (Deuteronomy 26:10-11 Knox).

God is not a kill-joy. He delights in family gatherings—fun, family, fellowship, friendship, and feasting on the good food He created. Bring the children, grandchildren, and friends—the more the merrier.

And remember, God doesn't want to be left out. He wants to be in the midst. Deuteronomy 27:7 Knox says, *"Eat and make good cheer **in the Lord's presence.**"*

God loves to be in your celebrations. Plan many! *Nancy*

Not Too Busy to Cuddle

I find that some days it is better to focus on what you didn't do. Today I did not become overwhelmed trying to accomplish too much. I did not place unrealistic expectations on anyone else, and I did not get too busy to sit down and cuddle.

Sometimes it is what you did not do that really counts! *Michelle*

- November 19 -

Forever Unchangeable

Psalm 119:89 says, *"Forever, O Lord, Thy word is settled in heaven."* That's it! It's settled! It's unchangeable, from the first command in Genesis to the last command in Revelation and everything in between!

God's first words to mankind were *"Be fruitful, and multiply, and replenish the earth"* (Genesis 1:28) and His last were *"If any man shall take away from the words of the book of this prophecy, God shall take away his part out of the book of life"* (Revelation 22:19).

We can belittle (because we don't take time to read it), resist, or disobey, but it doesn't change God's Words. They stand for all eternity. May we and each of our children reverence and obey these eternal decrees. *Nancy*

Showering With Love

My husband has been really going above and beyond the call of duty around here lately. It is much easier to shower love and praise on loved ones when they are blessing us, isn't it?

I need to work on showering love and praise each day, regardless of actual behavior. After all, God does not wait for me to be loveable before He showers me with His love. Let's pour on the love and praise today! *Michelle*

- November 20 -

God Laughs!

Someone asked me recently, "How do I respond to folk who think large families are a drain on the environment?" Who are they listening to? Humanistic garbage? Or, the God who created the earth?

Let's hear from God, *"For thus saith the Lord that created the heavens; God himself that formed the earth and made it; He hath established it, He created it not in vain, HE FORMED IT TO BE INHABITED: I am the LORD; and there is none else"* (Isaiah 45:18).

Maybe, like me, you have driven from the west to the east of USA. You drive for miles and miles and miles with no inhabitants, pass through a city, and continue the same pattern. The world is still waiting to be inhabited. *Nancy*

Reason to Bow our Knees

We delight naming our babies, don't we? We give it so much time, thought, and love!

We read in Ephesians 3:14, *"For this cause I bow my knees unto the Father of our Lord Jesus Christ, of whom the whole family in heaven and earth is named."* This verse reminds us that the Father has named us (Revelation 2:17).

How wonderful to remember His love for us. It certainly is cause to bow our knees. *Michelle*

- November 21 -

Fight Tooth and Nail

Proverbs 28:4 says, *"They that forsake the law praise the wicked: but such as keep the law contend with them."*

It's not enough to know that something is wrong in God's sight. If we love God's truth, we'll do something about it. We'll contend for the truth. We'll fight for it tooth and nail! We'll strive against evil.

"Who will rise up for me against the evildoers? Or who will stand up for me against the workers of iniquity?" (Psalm 94:16). *Nancy*

God Controls the Womb

The Bible is clear on who creates or takes away life.

* Genesis 16:2, *"Sarai said unto Abram, 'Behold now, the Lord hath restrained me from bearing.'"*
* Genesis 29:31, *"The Lord opened her* (Leah's) *womb."*
* Genesis 30:2, *"Jacob said, 'Am I in God's stead, who hath withheld from thee the fruit of the womb?'"*
* Ruth 4:13, *"The Lord gave her conception, and she bare a son."*
* Isaiah 44:2, *"The Lord that made thee and formed thee from the womb."*
* Isaiah 44:24, *"He that formed thee from the womb."*

The Lord grants life according to His plan and purpose. Why would anyone want to interfere with that? In addition, why would anyone judge if a womb is left in the hands of the Lord, and is often opened or is perpetually closed? The Lord can be trusted to know what is best, all the time, for everyone. *Michelle*

- November 22 -

Habitual Language

What language do you speak in your home? Ephesians 5:4 tells us that *"thanksgiving"* should be our dialect. Way's translation says, *"Let your language be all thanksgiving."* Spontaneous thankfulness to God and to one another should be the principal language of our home.

Make it a family project, and try it for one day! No complaining and groaning—thankfulness instead. No accusations and blame—thankfulness and appreciation instead! Then, seek to make it the habitual language of your home. *Nancy*

Ten Praises for Your Husband

In Song of Solomon 5:9, the daughters of Jerusalem ask the Shulamite woman, *"How is your beloved better than others?"* and she answers with no less than 10 praises of her man! They were all based on his physical glory, and she didn't even begin on his character qualities!

I was challenged by this and decided today I must find 10 praises to vocalize to my man. Would you like to accept this challenge, too? *Michelle*

- November 23 -

Inexhaustible Well

Is your love running thin? You may feel there is nothing much left in your marriage relationship. Can I tell you a secret? God's well of love never runs dry. It is inexhaustible.

The Message Bible paraphrase of Psalm 107:1 says, *"His love never runs out!"* What great news! When you have nothing left, draw from God's inexhaustible well.

Don't be concerned about your feelings. Thank God for His love, which fills your heart—and in faith and action, love with His love. You can do it! Yes you can, even when you have no feelings left!

Romans 5:5 says, *"The love of God is shed abroad in our hearts by the Holy Ghost which is given unto us."* Nancy

Consider Others Better Than Yourself

It may feel natural to focus on the negative, especially when looking at others, but the yield is bitter! Today I am challenged by Philippians 2:3-8 NASB, *"With humility of mind regard one another as more important than yourselves; do not merely look out for your own personal interests, but also for the interests of others. Have this attitude in yourselves which was also in Christ Jesus, who, although He existed in the form of God... emptied Himself, taking the form of a bond-servant... humbled Himself by becoming obedient to the point of death."* Words of life for me today. *Michelle*

They're Being Recorded

Did you know that the walls of your home recall the words that are spoken—the good and the bad? They affect the atmosphere of your home. That's scary, isn't it?

When Joshua gave his farewell speech to the children of Israel before he died, he set up a big stone and said, *"This stone shall be a witness unto us; for it has **heard all the words** of the Lord which He spake unto us."* (Joshua 24:27) If stones and walls can hear words, how much more must our words affect the tender hearts of our children? *Nancy*

No-Flop Recipe

Here is my recipe for a great day:

One part meaningful prayer
One part unconditional love
One part genuine thankfulness
One part selfless kindness
One part willing service
One part patience

Mix it all up into others-centeredness, seasoned with faith and trust. The result is a no-flop, praise-filled day! *Michelle*

- November 25 -

Keep Rejoicing

"Rejoice in the Lord always: and again I say, Rejoice" (Philippians 4:4). Of course, you know this Scripture. You know it so well that you often forget what it is saying.

I want to remind you that the joy of the Lord doesn't change just because you feel lousy. It is still the same. It is always available because Christ, who lives in you, is Joy. Therefore, keep rejoicing.

Rejoice that you are a child of God. Rejoice that you have eternal life. Rejoice that God has blessed you with your precious children. Rejoice that you trust in a God who will never fail you. *Nancy*

Soul Treasure

During our morning devotions today, I was explaining to our children the concept of storing up treasures in heaven (Matthew 6:20). I asked them what kind of treasure they thought they could take to heaven. Their favorite toy? No! The best treasure to take to heaven is another soul! When couples are open to receive children, there is hope for bringing "soul" treasure to heaven with them.

Why do folks waste time trying to gain more and more material treasure and yet think they cannot afford "soul" treasure? We are told to store up heavenly treasure, yet we fill our houses with clutter, which keeps us busy and disorganized. We have things so backwards, don't we? This was the lesson from our breakfast table today. *Michelle*

- November 26 -

What Is My First Response?

When Jesus was moved with compassion towards the hungry people who came to listen to Him, He asked Philip where they could buy bread to feed them all. Philip replied that eight months' wages would not buy enough bread for all the thousands of people (John 6:7).

I think that would have been my reply, too!

Like me, Philip looked at the situation; they had no money, and even if they did, where could they get enough food to feed this multitude? But Philip hadn't yet learned to look past his situation and circumstances and look to the Lord.

I pray that I will learn to look to the Lord first. How about you? *Nancy*

New Every Morning

"Thank you, Lord, for not treating us as our sins deserve. Your love is new every morning. That is the encouragement our weary souls need. You bless us with all we have need of and so much more. Amen." *Michelle*

- November 27 -

Consecrated Hands

God told Moses to consecrate the hands of Aaron and his sons, the priests. Exodus 28:41 Knox translation says, *"And thou shalt consecrate their **hands, and set them apart to serve Me** in the priestly office."* God has made us *"kings and priests unto our God"* and wants us to also have consecrated hands.

Consecrate your hands to the Lord as you use them to cook, clean, change diapers, and do all your household tasks. Think of them as being "set apart" to the Lord as you serve in your home. Know that you are doing a priestly work as you use your hands to love, nurture, caress, and hold your babies and children. *Nancy*

Daily Goals

Is your house immaculate with everything in perfect order? Do you always prepare the healthiest, organic meals imaginable? Do your children impress folks with their behavior and appearance?

These are all great, but sometimes we focus on outcomes rather than our daily, obedient life as a wife and mother.

Titus 2:3-5 NIV admonishes the older women to *"train the younger women to love their husbands and children, to be self-controlled and pure, to be busy at home, to be kind, and to be subject to their husbands, so that no one will malign the word of God."* These are the daily goals that need our focus the most. *Michelle*

- November 28 -

Our Only Glory

Is the cross of Jesus Christ the preeminent theme of your home? Do your children know, without doubt, that it is only by embracing the cross of Jesus that we have hope in this life and the next?

Paul confessed, *"God forbid that I should glory, save in the cross of our Lord Jesus Christ, by whom the world is crucified unto me, and I unto the world"* (Galatians 6:14).

What is honored most in your home—the cross of Christ or the things of this world?

> *The cross: it takes our guilt away;*
> *It holds the fainting spirit up;*
> *It cheers with hope the gloomy day,*
> *And sweetness ev'ry bitter cup.*

May the cross overshadow everything we do and say in our home this day and every day. *Nancy*

A Husband's Love

My husband says, "The closest thing to defining eternity here on earth is the amazing love of a man for his wife!" Yes, God intended marriage to be that way! *Michelle*

Never Going Under

Are you having a rough day? Be encouraged by Paul's confession, *"Always 'going through it,' yet never 'going under.' We know sorrow, yet our joy is inextinguishable. We have 'nothing to bless ourselves with' yet we bless many others with true riches. We are penniless, and yet in reality we have everything worth having"* (II Corinthians 6:10, J. B. Phillips).

You cannot go under when God is with you. His everlasting arms will never let you fall. Cry out to Him, for He will hold you up. *Nancy*

Prayer Power

My husband was running so behind he was going to miss his flight. He would have arrived at the airport as the plane was taking off! The stress was high as he ran out the door. I gathered the nearest children; we stood together in a circle holding hands as we asked the Lord to keep Dad safe on the icy roads, make all things well, and to allow him to somehow catch the flight.

A few minutes later, Cam called to say he forgot his wallet and passport and raced back to get them. "That's it, he'll never make it now!" I thought to myself.

Almost an hour later, Cam called again to say his flight was delayed by half an hour, and he would make it! I told him how we had prayed and felt ashamed of my disbelief. I was glad I hadn't voiced my doubts to the children. They got to see firsthand the amazing power of prayer. *Michelle*

- November 30 -

Daily Invitation

Revelation 21:3 says, *"And I heard a great voice out of heaven saying, Behold, the tabernacle of God is with men, and **He will dwell with them**, and they shall be His people, and God Himself shall be with them, and be their God."*

How amazing! God not only wants to dwell in our hearts, but He also wants to live in our homes. He wants to fill our homes with His presence—the atmosphere of His love, longsuffering, joy, and peace.

As you start each day, invite the King of kings to come into your home and fill every room with His holy presence. *Nancy*

Powerful Profession

"To nourish children and raise them against the odds is, in any time, any place, more valuable than to fix bolts in cars or design nuclear weapons" (Marilyn French).

I like this quote. Just as our affirming words never fall on deaf ears, but build up the hearers, so we mothers need affirming words to build us up, too. *Michelle*

- December 1 -

Building Tools

Proverbs 24:3-4 says, *"Through **wisdom** is a house builded; and by **understanding** it is established: and by **knowledge** shall the chambers be filled with all precious and pleasant riches."*

Three building tools are needed to successfully build our home—God's wisdom, understanding, and knowledge. In the midst of this deceived age, seek after God's wisdom and understanding. Search for God's knowledge, for it is foreign to the mindset of this world. Bathe yourself in God's Word, for it is only there you will find them. They may be different to the way of society, but the One who designed family knows the right tools for the job. *Nancy*

Keep Quiet and Pray

My friend was upset because her husband claimed she was lacking in "grace." She said not one thing and prayed about it instead. Days later, her husband praised her and said he had been wrong about thinking she didn't have "grace" and that she had the most "grace" of anyone he had ever met!

Are you upset about something? PRAY—and watch how amazingly God will deal with it! *Michelle*

- December 2 -

Speak His Name Today

How often does the name of Jesus fall from your lips during the day?
How often do your children utter the name of Jesus? His name brings
salvation. His name brings healing. His name brings deliverance.

Acts 4:12 says, *"Neither is there salvation in any other: for there is
none other name under heaven given among men, whereby we must be
saved."*

I love the words of the old hymn by John Newton,

> *How sweet the Name of Jesus sounds*
> *In a believer's ear!*
> *It soothes his sorrows, heals his wounds,*
> *And drives away his fear.*
> *It makes the wounded spirit whole,*
> *And calms the troubled breast;*
> *'Tis manna to the hungry soul,*
> *And to the weary, rest.*

Speak His name often today. *Nancy*

Serving is Joy

Oh the joy of serving! The right attitude makes life so sweet! May you
find joy in serving today! And may God fill you so that you can pour
His life into your husband, children, and the lives of others! *Michelle*

- December 3 -

A Good Sign

I was talking to a devoted young mother recently. She complained that her seven-month-old baby will not go to anyone else but her.

"This is a sign of good mothering," I encouraged her. When a baby is one-eyed to the mother, it shows that the two are well-bonded. That is a good thing!

Babies can get used to being cared for by others. It may make an easier life for the mother, but that is not what God planned for your baby. Don't get upset if your baby only wants you. Mother and baby are meant to be inseparable! *Nancy*

Combat the Lies

I heard the lyrics of a song today, "All we have to do is take these lies and make them true." How typical that is of our culture, trying to make lies into truth.

Do not be on the defense when you are standing for truth. Be on the offence! Proclaim truth to combat the lies in your home and everywhere you go. Especially proclaim truth regarding marriage and children! *Michelle*

- December 4 -

They Trusted

David confessed that his ancestors trusted in the Lord. Psalm 22:4-5 says, *"Our fathers **trusted** in Thee: they **trusted**, and Thou didst deliver them. They cried unto Thee, and were delivered: they **trusted** in Thee, and were not confounded."*

Did you notice that the words "they trusted" occur three times in two little verses? I would love to think that the generations to come in my family could have this testimony about me!

I want to daily trust Him in the little things that happen. In this way, I'll be able to trust Him in the bigger things. May this be our testimony. *Nancy*

Your Divine Purpose

Your great task of serving your family and building up your godly home is an eternal career. It will make an impact down through the generations. Do not be weary or discouraged. You are created for times such as these, and you are doing great. God would not have put you there if it weren't your calling! *Michelle*

- December 5 -

God Followers, Not Crowd Followers

Isaiah 59:14-15 NASB tells us that *"Justice is turned back, and righteousness stands far away; for truth has stumbled in the street, and uprightness cannot enter. Yes, truth is lacking."*

This picture fits our society today. However, I want to encourage you, mother, that in the midst of deception, you are raising children to be strong in God's truth.

Strengthen yourself in God, and rise up to the task. You have a powerful assignment. Be constantly on guard to push back the adversary who would come after your children. Pray over them. Fill them with truth. Immerse them in God's Word. Inspire them to be fearless warriors for God's justice and truth. Give them courage to be God followers instead of crowd followers. *Nancy*

Not Without Cost

Do you have goals in mind that seem too hard to reach? Perhaps you have a personal fitness goal or a character-changing goal. Every goal comes with a cost. They do not come for free.

Jesus Christ paid a huge cost to gain the reward of eternal salvation for us. Remembering how Jesus suffered to attain His goal motivates me to pay whatever is required to reach my goals. *Michelle*

- December 6 -

An Eternal Career

Ecclesiastes 3:11 tells us that God planted eternity in the heart of each human being. Every new baby is an eternal being. There is no greater privilege in life than to cooperate with God and be available to Him to bring into the world an eternal being that will live forever.

Everything else we pursue in this life will be left behind. All we will take into eternity with us, apart from our own redeemed soul, are the redeemed souls of our eternal children.

Mother, you are involved in an eternal career. Don't give up this high calling for anything less. *Nancy*

Hold My Tongue

"The fruit of the Spirit is love, joy, peace, patience, kindness, goodness, faithfulness, gentleness, and self-control" (Galatians 5:22-23 NASB). Prayer and God's Word are the starting point as we seek to increase fruit bearing in our lives.

I must admit that one of the best ways for me to be more patient, gentle, and self-controlled, not to mention kind, is to hold my tongue—even for a few moments! This helps me to think clearly, listen closely, or absorb the situation more fully. It also affords a moment to seek the Lord for help, and I am better equipped to handle whatever the situation at hand. *Michelle*

My God Is Enough

Are you feeling a little overwhelmed today? Do you feel weak and inadequate? Don't worry!

It doesn't matter if your strength is weak. The God in whom you believe is the God you can trust! When you are weak, He is your Rock on which to lean. When you are afraid, He is your Strong Tower in which to hide. When you face "the heat" and troubles, He is your Shelter and Protection. He is your Fortress when you feel you are failing. He is your Deliverer when no man can help. He is your Refuge when you are fainting. He is your Defense from the ravaging of the adversary.

You have all you need in your "God who is Enough." *Nancy*

Change the Direction

Nehemiah 8:10 reminds us that *"the joy of the Lord is your strength,"* but many things in life attempt to rob us of our joy. How do we keep a joyful attitude and a joy-filled atmosphere in our home?

I pray, but I also create a change of atmosphere when things are moving in the wrong direction. I may step outside for a bit to get some fresh air with the children, play some lovely music that lifts our spirits, or we may simply change our activity.

Sometimes, all that is needed is a small shift to see more joy flowing in our homes. It may even be a small shift in Mom's attitude to bring the joy back to the whole family! *Michelle*

- December 8 -

A Blow to the Enemy

Psalm 8:2 says, *"Out of the mouth of babes and sucklings hast Thou ordained strength because of Thine enemies, that Thou mightest still the enemy and the avenger."*

Isn't it amazing that God has chosen to use children to silence the enemy? Every new life that you bring into this world is a blow to the enemy who hates life! Never underestimate the power of little children to be used by God. *Nancy*

Vessel of God's Love

I like to ponder the fruit of the Holy Spirit listed in Galatians 5:22-23 and try to deliberately concentrate on one at a time. This makes it more manageable for me and easier to train our children. Focusing on one particular fruit at a time allows me to be more aware of how we are displaying it from day to day.

There are so many ways to show more love to those around us, aren't there? My husband loves a hug and a kiss as I walk by. One of my daughters particularly loves my full and undivided attention as she tells me a story. A few of the children love it when I do an errand on their behalf, while some prefer a treat or tiny gift. So many different love languages—so many opportunities!

May love abound in our homes today. Let us be vessels of God's love to make everyone feel loved and cherished. *Michelle*

- December 9 -

How Can I Doubt?

I am in awe of God. I love Him with all my heart. And yet, I am appalled at how often I fail to trust Him. How could I ever doubt for one minute the Supreme Potentate of the universe who created the worlds and upholds them by the word of His power?

Arthur W. Pink writes, "No prayer is too hard for Him to answer, no need too great for Him to supply, no passion too strong for Him to subdue, no temptation too powerful for Him to deliver from, no misery too deep for Him to relieve."

In your mind, your situation may look hopeless, but nothing is impossible to God. Trust in His omnipotent power to work on your behalf. *Nancy*

Accept With Grace

I saw this pinned up in a friend's garage: "Things turn out best for the people who make the best out of the way things turn out."

I have found that this to be true! When I accept with grace whatever happens in the day, knowing that my God is sovereign, I am way less stressed and way more able to bless. How about you? *Michelle*

- December 10 -

What's for Supper?

Isn't it amazing that even in His eternal heavenly home, God thinks about feeding us? Revelation 7:17 says, *"The Lamb which is in the midst of the throne shall feed them, and shall lead them unto living fountains of waters."*

Are you thinking about feeding your family? What are you going to prepare for them for your evening meal? It is not irrelevant. It is godly to think about feeding your family. And it is more than physical food.

Think about how you will feed their souls and spirit, too. What subject will you discuss at the table this evening? What questions will you ask the children? Are you preparing to make sure you have time for Family Devotions where you will feed their spirit? This is the most important nourishment you will give at your table this evening. *Nancy*

My Vision

I have a decoration hanging in my home that is as a symbol of my motherhood. I'm in the middle, and all the children I have and hope to have are in the circle around me. To complete the circle of 20, I ambitiously hope to have four more children in my forties. So far, I have 11 on earth and six in glory.

My three-year-old son, while looking at it yesterday, asked, "Are they with God?"

I replied, "Yes, they are!" It helps to make our entire family concrete. Imagine the circles I'll need for all the grandbabies! *Michelle*

- December 11 -

Sweet Odors

Song of Solomon 4:11 NLT says, *"The scent of your clothes is like that of the mountains and the cedars of Lebanon."*

In Bible times, the Oriental women perfumed their clothes with essential oils and spices. As they walked, they would release sweet odors to their husband and everyone in the home.

Why don't we think of doing this more? I am sure that not only husbands, but children would love it, as well.

Of course, more than physical fragances, our families are blessed by the aroma of Christ emanating from our lives. *Nancy*

The Children Are Listening

Today, my 10-year-old daughter said, "Mom, I am so glad you didn't listen to those people that said not to have so many children!"

Yes, the children hear all the comments. I think people forget about the underlying message of those comments when they speak them. We feel privileged to be raising "more than the average" number of arrows, and the children love it, too! *Michelle*

I will come!

God says, "I will come!" Do you want God to come to you? He comes into your life when you invite Him (Revelation 3:20). He comes to deliver you when you cry out to Him (Romans 10:13). He is coming again to take us to His eternal home (John 14:1-3).

But, there is another way He comes. Romans 9:9 NASB says, *"For this is the word of promise, 'At this time will I come, and Sarah shall have son.'"* Sarah did not have a son of her own accord. God had to come to her first! We cannot have conception without God coming. God comes to you when you conceive a baby.

How amazing, awesome, and incredible to think back on the times when God visited you and you conceived a baby by His will and power. Perhaps He may come to you again! *Nancy*

Thankful and Content

One of my favorite quotes of Nancy's is, "Wherever you are, dear mother, be there!" Very sound advice to us all!

May we all appreciate exactly where we are today, thankful and content to be where the Lord has placed us. Enjoy this day to the fullest. *Michelle*

- December 13 -

Teach Them How to Fight

Did you know that God wants each new generation to learn how to fight? He left enemies in the land of Israel so that each new generation of Israelites could be taught the art of war (Judges 3:1-3). While we are on this earth, we will always be in a battle. We are in a battle between the kingdom of God and the kingdom of darkness, between truth and deception, and between light and darkness.

We must know how to fight these daily battles, but we must also teach our children how to fight the enemy. If we do not teach them how to properly use strategies of warfare against the enemy, they will fall prey to his attacks. We want to raise children who can fight the enemy and still remain standing after the fight! Read II Corinthians 10:4-5; Ephesians 6: 10-18; and II Timothy 2:3-4. *Nancy*

Your Jewels

Billy Sunday said, "I thank God for what mother's love has done for the world. Oh, there is power in a mother's trust. As surely as Moses was put in his mother's arms by the princess, so God puts babes in your arms, as a charge by Him to raise and care for. Each child is a jewel that belongs to God, and He gives it to you to polish for Him so He can set it in a crown."

No earthly jewel is worth more. *Michelle*

- December 14 -

A Bride Worth Winning

Although Ruth the Moabitess was a foreigner to Israel, she earned the testimony of being known as a *"virtuous woman"*—a woman of valor, strength, and courage. Boaz confessed, *"All the city knows thee for a bride worth the winning"* (Ruth 3:11 Knox).

Mother, we have the privilege of training daughters to be a *"bride worth the winning."* What a wonderful vision! Many young women today are not ready for marriage. They have been educated for the market place instead of the high calling of motherhood and managing a home. But, we can prepare daughters who understand their destiny and know that embracing children and establishing a godly family is the highest privilege upon which a woman can embark.

We are not only preparing a *"bride worth the winning,"* but a "nation strengthener." *Nancy*

Love Deeply

1 Peter 4:8 NASB says, *"Keep fervent in your love for one another, because love covers a multitude of sins."*

Love enables us to overlook and forgive other's shortcomings. Those that love us deeply are also able to overlook and forgive our faults. Amazing, isn't it? At times the sin is grave and in dire need of repentance in order for it to be overlooked. Although we cannot force repentance, we can still love in spite of all, because of the love that was first shown us (1 John 4:10, 19). *Michelle*

- December 15 -

Press On Harder

Nehemiah faced persecution on every hand. His adversaries tried every way to stop him from building up the gates and wall of Jerusalem that were broken down.

You are also in a building program and your adversary, the devil, does not want you to succeed in building either. He wants your marriage and family weakened.

What did Nehemiah do? Nehemiah 6:9 he says, *"They all made us afraid, saying, 'Their hands shall be weakened from the work, that it be not done. Now therefore, O God, strengthen my hands.'"*

Instead of caving into their plots against him, he cried out to God for strength to continue. The Knox translation says, *"I pressed on the harder."* The more his enemies came aginst him, the more he determined to finish the task. The Moffat's translation says, *"I applied myself with greater energy."*

When everything is coming against you, don't give in. Press on harder in God's strength. *Nancy*

Choose to Rejoice

Why muddle in a puddle of despair when you can instead choose to find something to rejoice about? You are handpicked by our great God for this time and place, and He is never taken by surprise! Focus on the praiseworthy portions of your day. Even in the fiercest of trials, there is still plenty to praise! *Michelle*

- December 16 -

Full Time Career

Isaiah 54:13 says, *"And all thy children shall be taught of the Lord; and great shall be the peace of thy children."*

What a wonderful promise this is to claim and to pray for your children. However, you need to do your part. God gives you the responsibility, on His behalf, to teach your children His ways (Deuteronomy 6:6-9 and Proverbs 6:20-24). The word "taught" in the Hebrew means "trained, skilled, and discipled."

This sounds like a fulltime career, doesn't it? *Nancy*

Bless Your Enemies

Who wouldn't like a blessing? Who doesn't want to inherit a blessing? We all do, right?

I Peter 3:8-9 tells us exactly what to do. Offer blessing to others, even in the face of the evil they do to you. Love, have compassion, be courteous, and have pity on others. This not only allows us to inherit a blessing, but blesses our recipients.

Here is the Scripture: *"Finally, be ye all of one mind, having compassion one of another, love as brethren, be pitiful, be courteous: Not rendering evil for evil, or railing for railing: but contrariwise blessing; knowing that ye are thereunto called, that ye should inherit a blessing."* Michelle

- December 17 -

Making Many Rich

Do you consider yourself poor? Can't pay the bills? Your house is too small? You are in the very situation to make many people rich. II Corinthians 6:10 says, *"As sorrowful, yet always rejoicing; as poor, yet making many rich; as having nothing, and yet possessing all things."*

You make your husband rich by making your home a sanctuary of love, joy, and contentment. You make your children rich by giving them a godly heritage and showing them how to have a joyful attitude even in trials. You make them rich as you daily impart God's Word "richly" into their lives (Colossians 3:16).

What an amazing life! You can be as poor as a church mouse, and yet make people rich! Walk in the fullness of your divine-empowered life. *Nancy*

A Blessing to Be Needed

"Watch me, Mommy! Watch me, Mommy! Watch me, Mommy!" I heard this continuously at the pool, excitedly called from several of my children. At times, it felt overwhelming, maybe even slightly annoying. But then I realized how privileged I am to be "in demand."

How special it is that my children want me to see and be a part of all of their accomplishments. I want it to stay that way! *Michelle*

- December 18 -

Growing into Manhood

We have recently made another tradition in our family—to take each grandchild out to dinner when they turn 13 years of age. We don't look upon this as a time of their becoming a teenager, but of moving into manhood.

We recently celebrated the birthdays of Crusoe, Bowen, and Arden. It is great to see these young boys maturing, taking on responsibility, and already planning what they are going to do with their lives. They don't think like normal teenagers; they think like mature people. As we sit at the table, they talk about their dreams and how they are going to secure land and begin their farming experiences.

They don't have time to waste with normal "teenage stuff." They have a vision and want to get on with life! *Nancy*

Victory Is Yours

It is so easy to get down on ourselves when we mess up, isn't it? It is easy to lose our focus and shift our attention to our short-comings. This generally leads to a sense of overall discouragement and defeat. Then, guess what? The enemy laughs; and we moan and groan.

Do not be fooled. It is an opportunity to do better next time, to not repeat the error, and to grow and change. See failure in its proper light and use it as an impetus to future success. Then the enemy will be the one moaning and groaning. Keep on keeping on. Victory is yours, because Christ is yours! *Michelle*

God Is With You in Battle

Isn't it nice when everything is peaceful and lovely? We would rather not be in a battle. But did you know that God leads us into battles?

Yes, it is God who has got you in this battle. Exodus 23:20 says, *"For mine Angel shall go before thee, and **bring thee in unto the Amorites, and the Hittites, and the Perizites, and the Canaanites, the Hivites, and the Jebusites: and I will cut them off.***" That's not one battle, but many!

But God does not send you into battles on your own. He is with you in the battle. He is with you to win. He promises, ***"I will cut them off."***

Are you fighting a battle and feeling discouraged? Thank God that He is with you. Acknowledge that with His help you will win and will cut off the enemy who is seeking to destroy your family. *Nancy*

Listen and Learn First

I read recently, "You could love anybody if you took the time to hear their story." It is very easy to judge about what we know very little.

"Dear, Father, help us to love our neighbor as ourselves. Help us to love, listen, and learn, rather than judge, jeer, and joke. Amen." *Michelle*

God Loves Humility

Every aspect of Jesus' birth was bathed in humility—His earthly parents who were poor, the place of His birth which was little and insignificant, and His dedication when Joseph and Mary brought turtle doves because they could not afford a lamb.

In the birth of Jesus, God revealed His true character. Although He is the God of the universe, King of kings, and Lord of lords, He is not too proud to associate with the lowly and meet the needs of His created ones. In fact, God hates pride and revealed this in every aspect of Jesus' birth. Our delight should be to *"walk humbly before our God."* Read Psalm 68:4-6; 107:41; 113:4-9 and Micah 6:8. *Nancy*

The Right Perspective

It is so easy to have the wrong focus! In Luke 7:39-47, the Pharisee dining with Jesus focused on all the wrong things. We can also focus on the sins of others (especially in our families), rather than recalling that those who have been forgiven much, love much. In hard times, we may question His timing or purposes, lose focus in our weakness and doubt, and forget how we are supposed to respond as His redeemed children.

"Lord, grant us repentant hearts and childlike faith. Help us to walk with clear focus and see things as You see them! Help us to love much as we have been forgiven much. Amen." *Michelle*

- December 21 -

Devastating Humility

As we enter this time of the year when we celebrate the birth of Jesus Christ (even though we know it is not the actual time He was born), J. B. Phillips writes, "What we are in fact celebrating is the awe-inspiring humility of God, and no amount of familiarity with the trappings of Christmas should ever blind us to it. God's intervening into human history came about with an almost frightening quietness and self-effacement, and as millions will testify, He will come once again with the same silence and the same devastating humility into any heart ready to receive Him."

We can never get away from the truth of humility. God associates with those who are humble, but He opposes from the proud. *Nancy*

Your Words Are Powerful

Proverbs 12:18 states, *"The tongue of the wise promotes health."*

Our words are so powerful. They can change the course of a day—or even the course of a life!

Do you feel that your words aren't making much of a difference? Think again! Your tongue is a powerful tool of blessing to impart wisdom, grace, love, and health. Watch and wait for the results. *Michelle*

- December 22 -

Jesus Loves His Sheep

After the amazing experience of seeing the multitude of angels praising God, the shepherds decided to go to Bethlehem and see the Savior who had been born (Luke 2:15-16).

"Let's go!" they cried. Did they go alone? Oh, no! The shepherds would not have left the sheep, vulnerable and alone to be attacked by animals. In the Middle East, the sheep always follow the shepherd as he leads them. They are inseparable.

This is a true picture of Christ, the Good Shepherd, and we who are His sheep. Nativity scenes often show one or two sheep, but there would actually have been many sheep around Jesus. There wasn't only one shepherd, but a number of shepherds, each with their own flock.

As the sheep and the lambs surrounded the Lamb of God at His birth, so He still wants His sheep around Him. He wants them to be close enough to Him to hear His voice as He speaks to them. Gather your lambs close around you and snuggle in close to your Shepherd. *Nancy*

A Daily Prayer

David prayed, *"Let the words of my mouth, and the meditation of my heart, be acceptable in Thy sight, O Lord, my strength, and my redeemer"* (Psalm 19:14).

"Dear Lord, may the meditations of my heart, the words of my mouth, and the works of my hands be pleasing in your sight, Lord, today and every day. Amen." *Michelle*

- December 23 -

God Looks for Shepherd Hearts

Just as the Bethlehem shepherds led their sheep to Jesus, we as mother shepherdesses should lead our flocks to Jesus. Am I leading my children to Jesus by His character, which they see in me? Am I truly showing them the way? Am I leading them to the Jesus of the Bible, rather than a Jesus of my own imagination?

God wants mothers and fathers to have shepherd hearts. It is interesting that God chose a carpenter to be the earthly father of His son. Like the shepherds, carpenters were not on the highest rung of the career ladder. Joseph was a humble man, but he had a father's heart. God would not have put His son into a family of a man who did not have a father's heart. God was more interested in this quality than in his profession.

Now, in our 21st century, God is still looking for father and mother hearts to nurture His sheep and lambs. This is more important to God than a high-powered career. *Nancy*

Who Should Have Babies?

Why do so many folks think things have to look or be a certain way, before a baby should be born? With that logic, Mary should not have had Jesus, Elizabeth should not have had John, and Leah, being unloved, should not have had any children!

Do not listen to the "wisdom" of the world. It will lead you astray. *Michelle*

- December 24 -

He Still Comes Today!

Joy to the world! the Lord is come:
Let earth receive her King;
Let every heart prepare Him room,
And heaven and nature sing!

How true are these words, not only when Jesus came over 2,000 years ago, but today. He came to this world as a little baby and took on our flesh and blood. He understands your needs and still comes to you today. He wants to come into your heart.

This One who was *"born to be King"* (Matthew 2:2) wants to come into your home and reign as King. May His presence fill your home today as you prepare for Him and make Him King! *Nancy*

Worth It All!

Feeling discouraged? Think of Mary and Joseph. They had to face the masses with a pregnancy before marriage. They had to travel long, hard days on a donkey, right when she was due to give birth. She had to deliver their firstborn in a stinky barn. They had to flee for their baby's life and move to a foreign country. It wasn't easy, but it was all worth it!

The same is true for us mothers. It is all worth it! *Michelle*

- December 25 -

Love So Amazing

What a great salvation has been given to us. What a Savior we have, who humbled himself to leave the heights of glory to come as a baby to this sin-sick world. He, who was God, became a man to save and deliver us from our sin and selfishness, to redeem us back to Himself, and to give us eternal life. Our only response can be...

> *Were the whole realm of nature mine,*
> *That were an offering far too small,*
> *Love so amazing, so divine,*
> *Shall have my soul, my life, my all.*

"Thank you, dear Lord Jesus Christ, for giving up your life to give me eternal life. Amen." *Nancy*

What's Reality?

How often we are deceived. We looked upon the Christ child and thought Him poor. We looked at pregnant Mary and thought her shamed. We looked at Job and thought him guilty. We looked at scenarios and thought them impossible. We looked at our own problems and thought them unsolvable. We looked at our daily lives and thought them insignificant.

"Oh, Lord, help us walk in truth. Help us to see the true reality for what it is. Please save us from deception. Amen." *Michelle*

They'll See It in Your Eyes

In an interview, Toni Morrison was asked how she had become a great writer. What books did she read? In what method did she train? She replied, "Oh, no, that is not why I am a great writer. I am a great writer because when I was a little girl and walked into a room where my father was sitting, his eyes would light up. That is why I am a great writer. There isn't any other reason."

What do your children see when they look at you? Delight? Encouragement? Or do they see frowning and disapproval? What they see is what they will be! *Nancy*

Creative Extremists

How do you like this quote? "The question is not whether we will be extremists, but what kind of extremists we will be... The nation and the world are in dire need of creative extremists."

Our mission is to be creatively extreme in a world of complacency—extreme in faith, love, mercy, grace, and forgiveness; all because of the extreme love and forgiveness granted to us by Jesus Christ. Our goal is to accomplish this mission by the power of the Holy Spirit with exuberance and joy. Be extreme, and raise creative extremists for God's army. *Michelle*

- December 27 -

Life-Givers

How blessed we are to have the gift of life. How blessed we are as mothers to have the privilege of bringing life into the world, not only life for this earth, but for the eternal realm. We were created to be life-givers. To cooperate with God in bringing into this life an eternal soul who will live forever, is a privilege beyond any other.

Life-giving is our glory. We teach our children the wonder of life. We teach them the preciousness and value of life from conception to the grave. We teach them how to enjoy life. We speak life-giving words to our husband, children, and everyone we meet. We prepare our family life-giving foods. We delight in life because "Christ who is our life" dwells in us (Colossians 3:4)

Wow! What an amazing mandate we have as life-givers! *Nancy*

Give a REAL Kiss!

Today, make sure that you hug and kiss (I mean really hug and kiss in a meaningful way), each one of your family members. I know that, all too often, I let these affectionate moments slip by as I deal with daily tasks, but today will be different! *Michelle*

- December 28 -

Guarding the Nation

Just as God is the *"keeper of Israel,"* in the same way we reveal His character to our children and to the world when we are the *"keeper of our home."* (Psalm 121 and Titus 2:3-5).

What a blessing it is to be the *"keeper of the home."* It means to watch and guard over our home and children. It is no small task.

As we keep our marriages and homes strong, we also keep the nation! The nation weakens when the home weakens. *Nancy*

Blessed to Serve

As a guest, I used to feel sorry for the woman of the house who was so busy serving her family and guests. She was always the last one to sit and eat. Now, I am that same woman in my own home, I see the other side. The gratification and sense of pride that comes from serving others and meeting their needs far outweighs the gratification of sitting and eating myself.

It feels good to "reign" in the kitchen, offering hospitality and serving others. Why did I ever pity those blessed women who were privileged to show such hospitality? Clearly, I was missing their blessing. *Michelle*

- December 29 -

Fill Your Home with Laughter

How much laughter fills your home? I'm sure the children are always laughing, but what about you and your husband? Statistics say that children laugh up to 300–400 times a day, whereas most adults only laugh about 15 times a day. I wonder if some adults laugh even that much!

I know that the stress of each day limits laughter, but is it because we are taking the stress on ourselves instead of walking in the strength and rest of the Lord?

The Bible is correct when it says in Proverbs 17:22, *"A merry heart doeth good like a medicine."* I am sure that the more we laugh, the healthier we'll be. Laughter reduces stress, lowers blood pressure, boosts the immune system, and releases endorphins. Perhaps we need to start laughing more.

Laugh with your children. Laugh at the little things that happen. Laugh at yourself. Enjoy the life God has given you in your home. *Nancy*

Nourish Yourself

When we eat nourishing food for our body and healthy spiritual food for our soul, we equip ourselves to serve our family. We expect police to know the law and surgeons to know anatomy. Likewise, we need to equip and prepare ourselves for our high-powered career.

Take time to nourish yourself spiritually and physically so that you can be a blessing, and be blessed! *Michelle*

- December 30 -

God Will Never Abandon You

Isn't it great that we don't have to worry about trying to get this, covet after that, keep up with the Joneses, or be concerned what people will say or do to us? Why? Because God has promised, *"I will never leave thee, nor forsake thee."*

I love the way William Barclay translates Hebrews 13:5-6, *"Never let the love of money dominate your life. Be content with what you have. God himself has said: 'I will never let go My grip of you; I will never abandon you.' If that is so, we can meet life fearlessly, for we can say: 'The Lord is my helper, I shall not be afraid. What can any man do to me?'"*

You may have faced difficult trials this year, but God never abandoned His grip upon you. Nor will He let go of His grip in this coming year, no matter what you face. When you begin to slip, He will hold on tighter. In the face of difficult times, you can meet life fearlessly, trusting your God who will never leave you or forsake you. *Nancy*

God Chose You

Are you struggling with rebellion in your home? Take heart, even God the Father had rebellious children, and who could parent better than He?

You are the best parent for your child. God chose you for the job and He will help you through! *Michelle*

- December 31 -

How Long?

For how long will God love you? Until the very end (Jeremiah 31:3 and John 31:1).

For how long will He guide you? Continually... until the very end (Isaiah 58:11 and Psalm 48:14).

For how long will He carry you? Until your hair is white with age (Isaiah 46:3-4).

For how long will He be with you? Until the end of time; He will never abandon you for one day (Mathew 28:20 and Hebrews 13:5).

For how long will His goodness and mercy follow you? All the days of your life (Psalm 23:6; 52:1; 105:5 and 136:1-26).

Then why are you filled with worry? *Nancy*

Dance in the Rain

My verse for the day is II Corinthians 5:15, *"And that He died for all, that they which live should not henceforth live unto themselves, but unto Him which died for them and rose again."*

Life isn't about waiting for the storm to pass; it is about learning to dance in the rain. May you dance today. *Michelle*

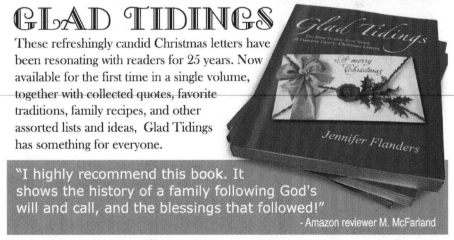

Made in the USA
Charleston, SC
17 February 2012